Positive Relationships in Sc

One of the five books in the *Mental Health and Wellbeing Teacher Toolkit*, this practical focuses on developing the skills necessary to build and maintain successful relationships. The book offers research-driven, practical strategies, resources and lesson plans to support educators and health professionals. Chapters span key topics including Communication, Respecting Yourself and Others, Resolving Conflict and Team Building. A complete toolkit for teachers and counsellors, this book offers:

◆ Easy-to-follow and flexible lesson plans that can be adapted and personalised for use in lessons, smaller groups or 1:1 work.

◆ Resources that are linked to the PSHE and Wellbeing curriculum for KS1, KS2 and KS3.

◆ New research, 'Circles for Learning', where the introduction of baby observation into the classroom by a teacher is used to understand and develop self-awareness, skills for learning, relationships, neuroscience and awareness of others.

◆ Sections on the development of key skills in communication, skills for learning, collaboration, empathy and self-confidence.

◆ Learning links, learning objectives and reflection questions.

Offering research-driven, practical strategies and lesson plans, *Positive Relationships in School* is an essential resource book for practitioners looking to have a positive impact on the mental health and wellbeing of the children and young people in their care: both now and in the future.

Alison Waterhouse has worked in mainstream, special education and the independent sector for the past 30 years, specialising in working with children with AEN including Mental Health and Wellbeing. She has set up and developed an Independent Therapeutic Special School, developed a role as Teacher in Charge of the Social and Emotional Wellbeing of the Whole School Community and has been an Inclusion Manager and Deputy Head in mainstream schools. She now works as an Independent Educational Consultant for SEN and Wellbeing, is involved in staff training and has her own Educational Psychotherapy practice. Alison works with children who are referred due to difficulties with self-esteem, anger, anxiety, depression and other Mental Health needs as well as children with learning differences. Alison is developing the 'Circles for Learning' Project in schools and has already undertaken a Primary Research Project and is now working on a Secondary Research Project. The resources were put together to support staff with these projects.

The invisible roots of learning

Emotional literacy

Self-discovery

Skills for effective learning in school

Positive relationships in school

The brain and learning

Positive Relationships in School

Supporting Emotional Health and Wellbeing

Alison Waterhouse

Routledge
Taylor & Francis Group

LONDON AND NEW YORK

First published 2020
by Routledge
2 Park Square, Milton Park, Abingdon, Oxon OX14 4RN

and by Routledge
52 Vanderbilt Avenue, New York, NY 10017

Routledge is an imprint of the Taylor & Francis Group, an informa business

British Library Cataloguing-in-Publication Data
A catalogue record for this book is available from the British Library

Library of Congress Cataloging-in-Publication Data
Names: Waterhouse, Alison, 1963– author.
Title: Positive working relationships in school : supporting emotional health and wellbeing / Alison Waterhouse.
Description: Abingdon, Oxon ; New York, NY : Routledge, 2019.
Identifiers: LCCN 2018060412 (print) | LCCN 2019011223 (ebook) | ISBN 9780429428081 (Ebook) |
    ISBN 9781138370296 (pbk) | ISBN 9781138370272 (pbk) | ISBN 9780429428081 (ebk)
Subjects: LCSH: Affective education. | Teacher-counselor relationships. | Students—Mental health.
Classification: LCC LB1072 (ebook) | LCC LB1072 .W373 2019 (print) | DDC 370.15/34—dc23
LC record available at https://lccn.loc.gov/2018060412

ISBN: 978-1-138-37029-6 (pbk)
ISBN: 978-0-429-42808-1 (ebk)

Typeset in Avant Garde
by Apex CoVantage, LLC

To three very special people: Jenny, Suzi and John, who have shown me what friendship truly is and who have always been there for the ups and downs of life, with a smile, glass of bubbly or a hug.

Contents

Introduction   xi

CHAPTER 1   Communication   1

Active listening   3

Body language   10

Facial expressions   16

The language we use   22

Thinking before you speak   26

Conversational skills   32

CHAPTER 2   Respecting yourself and others   37

Co-operation   39

Sharing and taking turns   42

No bullying, teasing or put-downs   45

Appreciate the benefits of diversity and celebrate difference   51

Treating people equally   55

Being assertive   59

Empathy: Walking in another person's shoes   65

CHAPTER 3   Friendship   69

Interactions   71

Co-operation   76

Respecting confidences   81

Positive feedback   87

Contents

	Acknowledge when you have made a mistake	94
	Being kind and thoughtful	99
	Being able to welcome the ideas of others	108
CHAPTER 4	Participation	113
	Taking part and having a go	115
	Including everyone	120
	Working together	127
	Building your confidence	134
	Resilience	140
	Focusing and concentration	144
CHAPTER 5	Resolving conflict	151
	Active listening	153
	Being open to new ideas	158
	Points of view	161
	Compromise	165
	Problem solving	170
	Recounting	175
	Persistence	186
CHAPTER 6	Team building and collaboration	191
	Respect	193
	Encouragement	198
	Accepting the opinions and ideas of others	202
	Flexibility	206
	Constructive feedback	211

Problem solving   217

Supporting others   221

Bibliography   227

Supporting others   221

Introduction

POSITIVE RELATIONSHIPS

As social beings, our ability and skill in forming and maintaining relationships is essential to us and our capacity to function within society. It is thus a key component of being mentally healthy and having a positive sense of wellbeing. Good relationships are the building blocks on which our futures are built and they are influenced from our earliest moments.

Stephen Jay Gould, an American biologist, put forward the idea that all babies are born prematurely – they are foetuses outside the womb (Gould 1992). If we think of babies in this way then we can think of the baby's brain at birth being considerably immature. We know that a baby's brain is a quarter of the adult size at birth. Birth triggers a burst of neural growth which is linked to the child's interaction with their caregiver. The baby's stress reactivity throughout life is literally being put together during its first few years. The neural systems that underpin language, emotion and social development, thinking and behaviour are all being wired in the early child-parent relationships.

Alan Schore (1994) suggested that positive looks are the most vital stimulus to the growth of the brain. When the carer smiles at the baby with love in their eyes this stimulates the release of endorphin and dopamine, both of which make the human body feel good. These hormones travel to the brain and cause it to grow. Negative facial expressions trigger the stress hormone cortisol to be released, which stops the secretion of endorphins, which in turn impacts on the growing brain. Many of the brains areas are not fully formed at birth and so their successful growth and genetic development depend on the amount of good experiences. By the end of the first year, a human baby has reached the level of development that other animals achieve at birth. By continuing its growth outside the human body, the human brain is influenced by the environment more than the brains of other animal, especially in the area of social interaction. These interactions with other people directly shape the growing mind of the baby (Siegel 2015). Interpersonal neurobiology (IPNB) is an interdisciplinary field that seeks to understand the links between our brain, mind and interpersonal relationships. IPNB hopes that with this approach it will be able to find new strategies that will develop understanding and promotion of wellbeing (Siegel 2015).

The systems that support our survival are all attuned to our environment, including the emotions and internal states of the people around. The Autonomic Nervous System (ANS) is constantly scanning to determine whether our environment is safe. When we sense the people around us are accepting, curious and accepting of us then we experience a sense of safety. If, however, we feel that the people around us are critical or hostile, our emotional scanner picks this up and places us on alert. When our body is on alert, our brain has shut down to learning and new experiences as it is in survival mode. Understanding the communication of emotions through body language and facial expressions is important in creating a safe classroom environment that promotes learning. Understanding the function of the brain in response to fear and danger supports teachers in understanding relationships and enables them to use their own body and brain to support the co-regulation of the children and young people (CYP) they are working with (Olson 2014).

Attachment Theory, proposed by John Bowlby, stated that human infants are biologically programmed at birth to seek and make emotional bonds with another. This attachment system, he argued, was an evolutionary mechanism to ensure survival of the infant (Maternal Care and Mental Health 1951). Bowlby demonstrated that, as mobility increases, the infant starts to feel safe enough to explore, confident in the availability of their primary carer at times of stress. He described this 'secure base' as vital to the containment of anxiety if exploration and new learning are to unfold. The capacity, sensitivity and ability of the mother to comprehend the anxieties set off by fear, uncertainty and distress he describes as a major aspect of early attachment experience.

Bowlby's Attachment Theory opened up an understanding of the importance of relationships in child development and created a shift in thinking that enabled an understanding of how behaviour is influenced by relationships and how important the early relationship is for a child to thrive.

Klein (1931) proposed that the way primary carer and baby come together in the earliest months of life and the way they negotiate the feeding relationship sets the scene for all other subsequent relationships, including the learning relationship.

Bion extended Klein's model of learning based on the interaction between mother and infant. He believed that the way in which the primary carer was able to connect with the infant's mind meant that the baby experienced containment for all their anxieties and projections. This later became his theory of Container Contained (1963). He put forward that the ability to learn and to think had its foundations in the meeting of minds of the mother – baby dyad.

Ainsworth went on to build upon Bowlby's work, devising the Strange Situation Procedure (Ainsworth &Wittig 1969). She found it was possible to identify specific patterns of behaviour for both mother and child. Three categories of insecure attachment were observed: Avoidant, Resistant/Ambivalent, and Disorganised (Ainsworth 2015).

Understanding how the brain develops in relation to others and how this impacts on future relationships is vital for teaching professionals. By developing our knowledge within this area we become more able to give CYP new relational experiences and develop a classroom environment that supports the building of positive relationships with others.

When the child engages with the learning task, they expect the same response as the one they experienced in their early relationships. If this experience was a positive one of being thought about, supported and having their emotions regulated, this becomes the expectation for the teacher and the school. If, however, this experience was one of not being understood or supported, where emotions were not contained, then it is this negative experience that the child expects. When children experience this, they learn to protect themselves and to do this they use a range of defence mechanisms whose function is to manage the anxiety that an internal conflict of desires has created. These defence systems, when triggered by learning, impact on the relationship between adult and child and impede learning. The initial deprivation of not having experienced a thinking-attuned adult means that the child is now not able to experience the opportunity of help and new learning. Williams calls this 'double deprivation' (Williams 1997).

Salzberger-Wittenberg et al. (1983) suggest that, when a child moves into school, the teacher and the school take the role of the containing parent and the secure base.

Much research has been undertaken looking at the student-teacher relationship (Minuchin and Shapiro 1983). This growing research highlights the unique contribution teachers can make to CYP's social, emotional and intellectual development throughout their school lives (Resnick et al. 1997).

Geddes (1999) explored cases of children being supported within school. From these she surmised that particular patterns of attachment could be observed through responses to both the teacher and the task. This led to the Learning Triangle model, relating learning patterns to attachment patterns (Geddes 2006).

THE CIRCLES FOR LEARNING PROJECT

Circles for Learning is a unique research-based, whole class or small group project that builds the positive foundations for Mental Health and Wellbeing. It supports and strengthens learning skills alongside the development of social skills, emotional literacy and wellbeing. It facilitates and encourages children to experience how learning happens and explore brain development, relationships and emotions. This includes how other people might feel or experience situations, how to manage emotions, discover our sense of self and understand how our beliefs influence our behaviour.

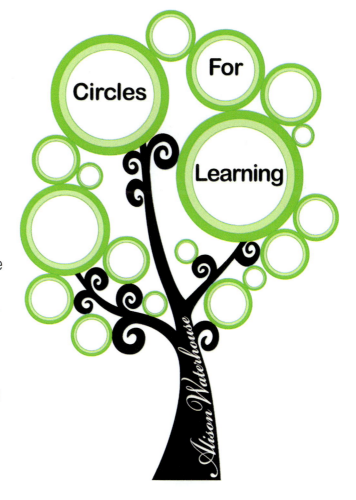

Circles for Learning has been developed by Alison Waterhouse over the past five years. Alison initiated the Circles for Learning Project in primary schools in East Sussex, where she led and developed this innovative way of working with children. As colleagues became aware of her work, they asked to get involved, so Alison set up the Primary Research Project for five schools in East Sussex where she worked closely with the class teachers to both design and develop the project in

their schools. This enabled her to work in both small rural schools and very deprived large urban schools as well as with a variety of teachers. As a result of the interest of professionals in the Secondary field, Alison has just completed a research project with 4 different secondary schools to explore and measure the impact of the work within their environment. This work has been the core of a research MA in Education with the University of York.

The project trains and then supports teachers to bring a parent and baby into the classroom once a month for a year. The children and young people are supported in observing the interactions, learning, relationships and the baby's early developing sense of self. Then, with the support of the teacher, they explore and think about what they have seen and how this may link to their own development, thinking, behaviour and ways of interacting with others.

These observations are the provocation or stimulus to follow-up work led by the teacher exploring one of the Circles for Learning's five areas of work:

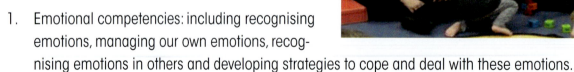

1. Emotional competencies: including recognising emotions, managing our own emotions, recognising emotions in others and developing strategies to cope and deal with these emotions.

2. Relationships: including social skills, the learning relationship, social inclusion and empathy.

3. Self-discovery: including self-concept, self-esteem, self-efficacy, self-regulation, self-talk, self-compassion, mindsets and resilience.

4. Skills for effective learning.

5. Neuroscience and learning.

These five key areas form the foundations for Mental Health and Wellbeing. The follow-up work is not a scheme of work to be followed regardless of the needs of the children or young people but a wide range of activities that the teacher can refer to and use that supports the needs of the group at that time.

The resources within each of the five books in the *Mental Health and Wellbeing Toolkit* can be used as standalone resources to support the five key areas that create the foundations for Mental Health and Wellbeing or as part of the Circles for Learning Project.

TRACKING SHEET

NAME/GROUP:		
DATE:	**TERM:**	
ASSESSMENTS UNDERTAKEN:	**OTHER INFORMATION:**	
Date	Lesson:	Comments
Date	Lesson:	Comments
Date	Lesson:	Comments
Date	Lesson:	Comments
Date	Lesson:	Comments
Date	Lesson:	Comments
Date	Lesson:	Comments
Date	Lesson:	Comments
Date	Lesson	Comments
Date	Lesson	Comments

Circular Tracking Document

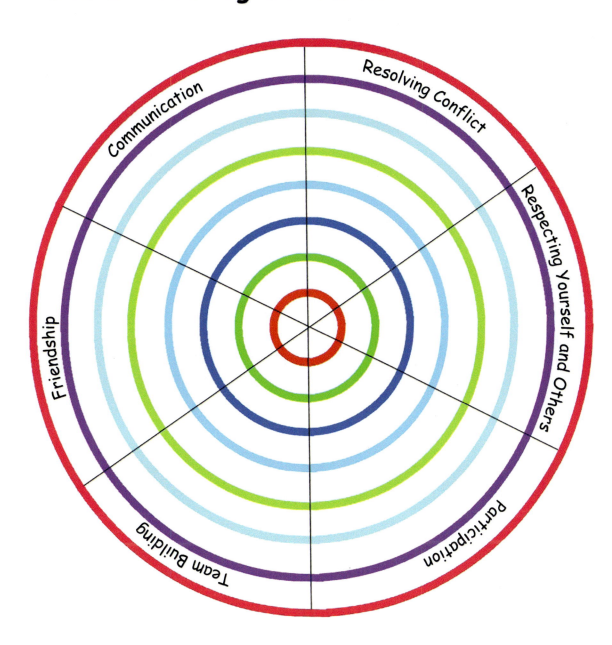

The circular tracking document has been designed to allow practitioners to monitor and track the areas that they have covered with the children. As each lesson is covered they are entered onto the document within the focus section. This enables practitioners to see the particular focus they are taking with their group. For some classes they may present a high need within a particular area or a strength in another area and so this can be shown and monitored. The document also allows for other lessons/activities to be added to the document that may have extended knowledge and understanding in this area from PSHE or Circle Time focus.

The document allows the flexibility to meet the needs of the children as they arise rather than having to follow a pre-set curriculum and in so doing allows practitioners to clearly see the areas of need and what they are doing to meet them.

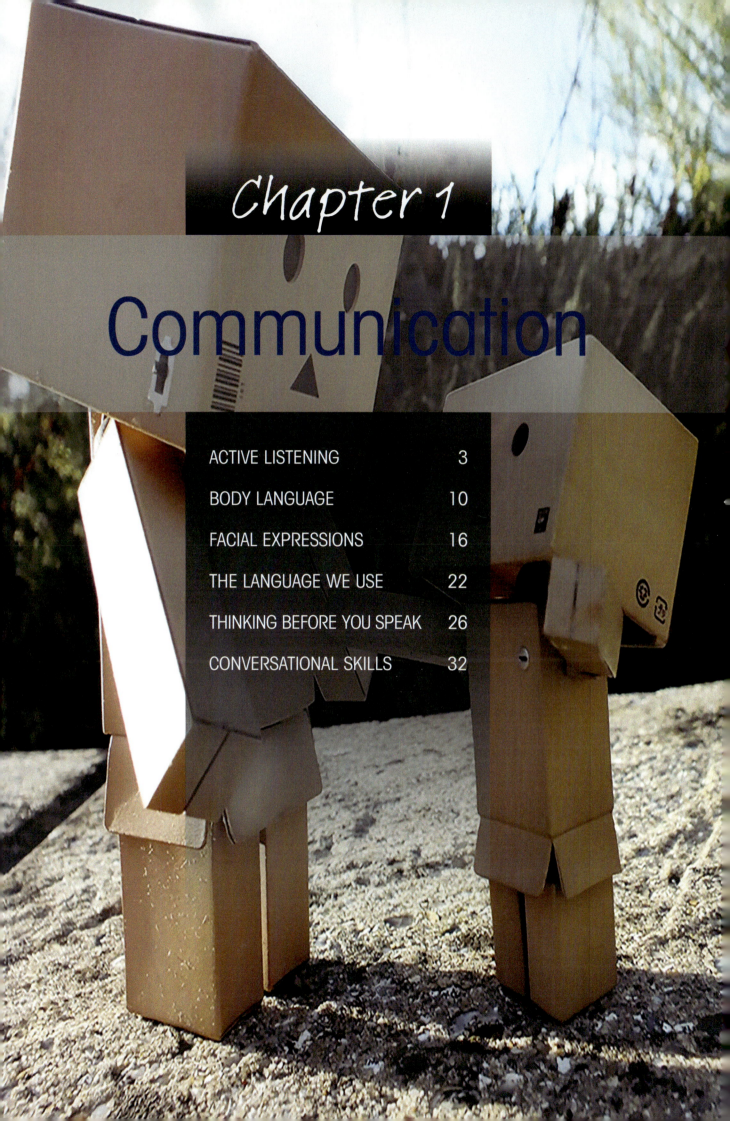

Chapter 1

Communication

ACTIVE LISTENING   3

BODY LANGUAGE   10

FACIAL EXPRESSIONS   16

THE LANGUAGE WE USE   22

THINKING BEFORE YOU SPEAK   26

CONVERSATIONAL SKILLS   32

Active listening

SESSION OBJECTIVES

To be able to listen to another person giving them their whole attention.

To be able to demonstrate some of the active listening skills of paraphrasing, not interrupting or adding own points of view etc.

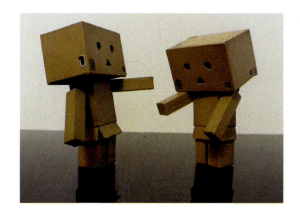

SESSION OUTCOMES

✓ To be able to listen to another person giving your full attention.

✓ To be able to describe what active listening is like.

✓ To be able to demonstrate active listening with another person.

LESSON PLAN

➢ Ask the children to remember a time when they watched their class parent trying to explain something to their baby.

➢ Describe what they saw and what they were doing.

For those classrooms not able to undertake the Circles for Learning Project, video clips or photographs can be used to support the discussion around the topic and stimulate thoughts and ideas from the children and young people.

Task

KS1: To share a telephone conversation with someone.

KS2/KS3: To be able to describe what active listening is and to demonstrate some of the features of this.

KS1

1. Demonstrate two people engaging in a conversation where the listener is distracted and not listening fully.

2. Discuss how the person talking is feeling.

3. Share with the children that you are going to actively listen to the person and ask them to 'Spot the Difference'.

4. Write a list of differences or things the children noticed.

5. Ask the children to work in pairs to demonstrate good listening skills whilst on the phone to a friend who is telling them all about their holiday.

6. Ask the person who was the listener to share 3 facts about the holiday after listening.

7. Ask the children to change over.

8. Share some of the experiences and ask the children to spot the skills and share these at the end.

KS2

1. Demonstrate two people engaging in a conversation where the listener is distracted and not listening fully.

2. Discuss how the person talking is feeling.

3. Share with the children that you are going to actively listen to the person and ask them to 'Spot the Difference'.

4. Write a list of differences or things the children noticed.

5. Ask the children to get into pairs and try out both active listening and poor listening.

6. Discuss how it feels.

7. Highlight the skills and behaviours used when actively listening to someone.

8. Ask the children to create a poster for the class to show how to actively listen to someone.

KS3

1. Demonstrate two people engaging in a conversation where the listener is distracted and not listening fully.

2. Discuss how the person talking is feeling.

3. Share with the children that you are going to actively listen to the person and ask them to 'Spot the Difference'.

4. Write a list of differences or things the children noticed.

5. Ask the children to get into pairs and try out both active listening and poor listening. Stop and ask children to demonstrate different points as they are seen.

6. Discuss together how it feels to be truly listened to and when the listener isn't really interested.

7. Ask the children to write a conversation on the phone/text between themselves and their best friend to show the language they would use to support their friend in managing a difficulty.

8. Share the phone conversation as an example and explore the different language used and how this influenced the conversation.

9. Highlight the neutrality of the friend throughout – discuss how hard this is but also how it helped, enabling the person to work through their anger and to a place where they had worked out what to do by themselves.

10. Ask the children to work in pairs. Discuss the sort of scenarios they could use (keep them simple) and come up with a phone script of their own.

11. Share and discuss.

RESOURCES

1. Telephones

2. A short passage about a topic being explored

3. Active Listening Highlights sheet

4. Active Listening Transcript

IMPORTANT POINTS

When we listen to someone talking with our whole mind and body they feel listened to and we are more likely to understand them more fully.

Active Listening is a skill that can be developed.

LEARNING LINKS

Speaking and listening, relationships, co-operation, team work, social competencies.

REFLECTION

Questions:

Positive comment from child:

Positive comment from adult:

LEARNING DIMENSIONS		SOCIAL & EMOTIONAL SKILLS	
Strategic awareness	🟧	Emotional literacy	🟩
Learning relationships	🟩	Neuroscience	
Curiosity		Self-regulation	
Creativity		Self-development	🟩
Meaning making			
Changing & learning			
Resilience			

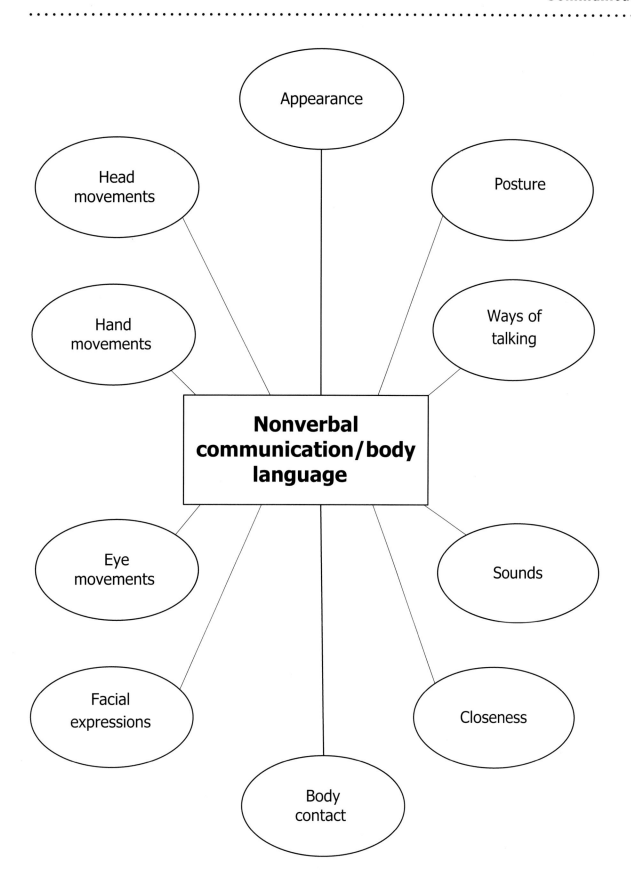

Appearance

Head movements

Posture

Hand movements

Ways of talking

Nonverbal communication/body language

Eye movements

Sounds

Facial expressions

Closeness

Body contact

GUIDE FOR ACTIVE LISTENING

1. Make eye contact when the other person is talking. Most of the time you should aim for eye contact to be about 60–70% of the time that you are listening.

2. Lean towards the other person and nod your head occasionally. This shows that you are interested and paying attention to what they are saying.

3. Avoid folding your arms as this body language signals that you are not listening – you shut them out with your folded arms.

4. Instead of joining in the conversation and saying what you think or feel, simply paraphrase what has been said. You might start this off by saying 'In other words, what you are saying is . . .'.

5. Do not interrupt while the other person is speaking.

6. Do not think or plan what you are going to say in return to their language. This ensures that if they say something at the end you have listened and taken this in – they may change their mind at the end of a conversation or add something important that you may miss if you have an answer ready.

7. In addition to listening to what is said, watch their other nonverbal actions. These will give you clues about what they are thinking or feeling as they talk. Other nonverbal actions are facial expressions, tone of voice, head movements, hand movements or their posture; these can sometimes tell you more than words alone.

8. While listening, stop your own thoughts and internal talk but avoid switching off or daydreaming. It is impossible to attentively listen to someone else and your own internal voice at the same time.

9. Show interest by asking them questions to clarify or help you understand what they are saying. Try and ask open-ended questions to encourage them to share more about what they are thinking or feeling. Try to avoid questions that only need a yes or no answer as these tend to make the conversation stop or lose its flow.

10. Try not to change what you are talking about as this makes the other person think that you were not listening to what they were saying or that you are not interested in their ideas or views.

11. As you listen, be open to what they are saying, listen properly to their ideas and views, try to be neutral, and withhold judgment about what they are saying.

ACTIVE LISTENING IN ACTION

The conversation below shows how active listening can make the speaker feel heard and understood. It helps them to open up and say more about what they think and feel and the reasons behind how they are thinking.

Sally: Hi Emma . . . I'm so sorry to phone you like this, but I've had a fight with my sister and I'm feeling really miserable as we haven't spoken since.

Emma: Hi Sally . . . no worries, it's fine, I'm glad you thought you could phone me. It's not a problem. So you had a fight and now you guys aren't talking to each other?

Sally: Yes . . . . we were arguing because I wanted to borrow her long black coat as I was going out and it looks so good, she'd said I could borrow it but then she said she had to wear it as she was going out with Roger. I was so cross as I was really looking forward to wearing it and I haven't got a decent coat as Mum said she was getting me one for my birthday next month. It was so unfair, especially as she has said yes and then just because of that stupid Roger she changed her mind. I got really mad and shouted at her and then stormed out, but now I feel bad, I said some really mean things at the time.

Emma: I hear you . . . you got really mad about her saying you couldn't borrow her coat when she had said you could and you shouted and got really angry and said some unkind things, but now you feel bad about it.

Sally: Yes, she just made me so angry, assuming that my going out wasn't as important as her date. She knew I hadn't got a coat as I had to wait for my birthday. I know her date with Roger was important but I thought that she would keep her word as she had said that I could wear it. I got so cross we couldn't talk about it anymore.

Emma: Sounds like you were angry because she went back on what she had said.

Sally: Totally. Maybe I should just tell her in a calm way how hurt and upset I was and that I know it is her coat but it was the breaking of a promise that upset me. I just don't like the fact that she is not talking to me as we normally get on so well and have a real laugh. She probably needs to know I am sorry for what I said and am sorry I got so angry with her – it's only a coat!

Emma: So . . . maybe you will talk to her and tell her you understand her feelings . . . and that you miss talking and sharing things with her.

Sally: Yes, that's what I think I will do. Thanks! I feel a lot better just having a chance to share what I was feeling.

Body language

SESSION OBJECTIVES

To understand that body language and facial expression are forms of communication.
To be able to identify simple facial expressions and link them with an emotion/feeling.

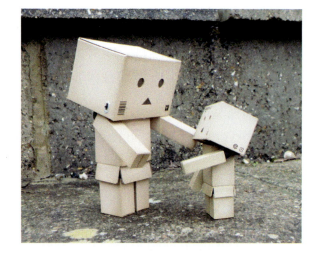

SESSION OUTCOMES

✓ To be able to use nonverbal communication to share a feeling.

✓ To be able to identify some aspects of nonverbal communication and explain what they convey.

LESSON PLAN

➤ Ask the children to remember a time when they watched their class parent interact with their class baby – what sort of communication did they use to convey how they felt?

For those classrooms not able to undertake the Circles for Learning Project, video clips or photographs can be used to support the discussion around the topic and stimulate thoughts and ideas from the children and young people.

Task

KS1: To be able to identify how someone is feeling by their body language and facial expression when playing 'How do I feel' charades.

KS2: To be able to create a Top 10 Tips for understanding nonverbal communication.

KS3: To be able to use nonverbal communication as a way of making someone feel that you have heard and understood what they are trying to say.

KS1

1. Show the children the 'For the Birds' video clip.

2. Discuss what the birds were feeling and why.

3. How do they know? There were no words spoken.

4. Discuss body language – what is it?

5. Ask the children to give some examples – using their bodies to send a message or feeling. Using their face to share an emotion.

6. Play 'How do I feel' charades. Cut up the tasks and fold them up and put them in a container. Do the same with the emotions, putting them in a different container. Ask a child to take one piece of paper from each and then act out the task in the way the emotion tells them to – this could be to hang out the washing in an angry way.

7. The other children have to guess the emotion and the task.

KS2

1. Show the children the 'For the Birds' video clip.

2. Discuss what the birds were feeling and why.

3. How do they know? There were no words spoken.

4. Discuss body language – what is it?

5. Ask the children to give some examples – using their bodies to send a message or feeling. Using their face to share an emotion.

6. Watch the nonverbal communication YouTube clip and discuss.

7. Ask the children to imagine that the class had a visitor from another planet – the alien has no idea about body language. Ask the children in pairs to create a Top 10 Tips for understanding body language.

8. Share the posters and explore which things are hard to understand.

KS3

1. Watch the Mr Bean shopping trip video.

2. Discuss how we know what is happening when so little is said.

3. Explore and discuss body language.

4. Watch nonverbal communication YouTube clip and the 'Tactics to Read Body Language' clips.

5. Ask the children to work in pairs and use the skills they have discussed on nonverbal communication to demonstrate listening to a friend talking about something that they enjoy.

6. Share the short presentations – ask the other children to count up how many different nonverbal ways of communicating they saw.

RESOURCES

1. 'How to read body language', www.youtube.com/watch?v=Nmp_-JByPaY

2. Nonverbal communication, www.youtube.com/watch?v=csaYYpXBCZg

3. 'How do I feel' charades activities and feelings sheet

4. Paper

5. Pens

6. 'For the Birds' animation, www.youtube.com/watch?v=IK13SWOQWO4

7. 'Shopping with Bean', www.youtube.com/watch?v=6IIPvYGex2s

8. Communication diagram

IMPORTANT POINTS

We communicate in a variety of ways; however, nonverbal communication is the most important way.

Nonverbal communication includes body language, facial expression, how we dress, posture, ways of talking, hand movements, eye movements and body contact.

LEARNING LINKS

Teamwork, co-operation, understanding others, social and emotional competencies.

REFLECTION

Questions:

Positive comment from child:

Positive comment from adult:

LEARNING DIMENSIONS		SOCIAL & EMOTIONAL SKILLS	
Strategic awareness	🟧	Emotional literacy	
Learning relationships		Neuroscience	
Curiosity		Self-regulation	
Creativity	🟩	Self-development	🟩
Meaning making	🟧		
Changing & learning	🟩		
Resilience			

Sad	Excited
Angry	Frustrated
Frightened	Hysterical
Worried	Thoughtful
Miserable	Disgusted
Frantic	Bored
Distracted	Panic
Calm	Cheerfully
Curiously	Impatiently
Irritated	Carefree
Bewildered	Anxious
Rage	Embarrassed
Manic	Tired
Carefully	Furious
Washing up	Making the bed
Washing the car	Hoovering the floor
Making dinner	Ironing
Eating dinner	Having a shower
Doing homework	Mowing the lawn
Dusting	Walking to the shops
Reading a book	Driving a car
Shopping	Digging the garden

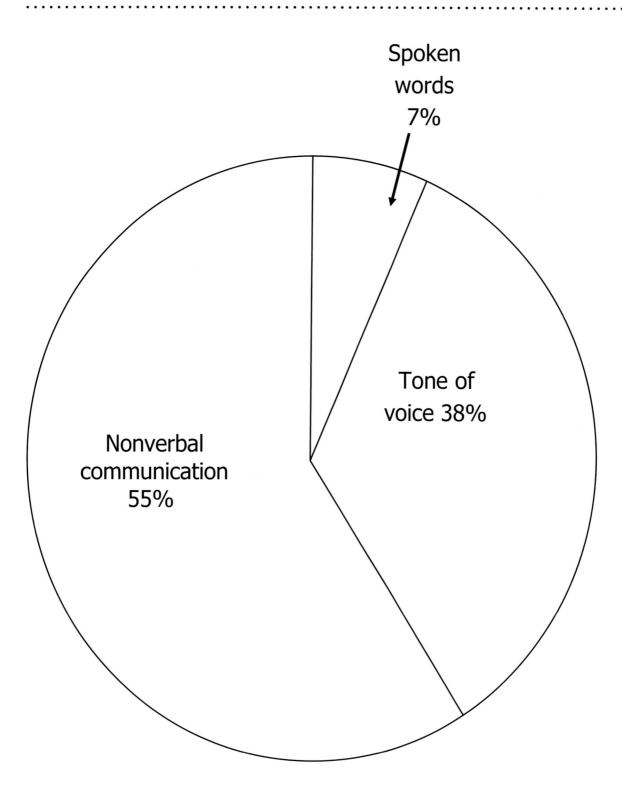

Spoken words 7%

Tone of voice 38%

Nonverbal communication 55%

Facial expressions

SESSION OBJECTIVES

To understand that we communicate by using our face and that sometimes we are not aware of this.

To understand and explore different facial expressions and what they mean.

SESSION OUTCOMES

✓ To understand different facial expressions and what they mean.

✓ To be able to use facial expressions to add to our communication with others.

LESSON PLAN

➢ Ask the children to watch a video of their class parent communicating with their class baby – discuss what they can see – how does the parent use their face to support what they are saying?

For those classrooms not able to undertake the Circles for Learning Project, video clips or photographs can be used to support the discussion around the topic and stimulate thoughts and ideas from the children and young people.

Task

KS1: To be able to recognise different facial expressions and link them to feelings.

KS2: To be able to recognise and discuss different facial expressions and link those to how people feel.

KS3: To understand that the most important way we communicate with others is via nonverbal communication, of which facial expressions are a huge part.

KS1: To make masks showing a variety of facial expressions.

KS2: To create verbal stories using a feelings dice.

KS3: To create dice with different facial expressions on the faces and then to use these to create verbal stories.

KS1

1. Read the story *The Saddest King* by Christopher Wormell.

2. Discuss with particular attention to the pictures.

3. Cut up the feelings labels and put them in a container. Ask the children to take turns to choose one. Do not let them show the others in the class. Once they have chosen one, ask them to put on this face and ask the others to guess what feeling they are showing with their face.

4. Take photos of the faces and label them.

5. Discuss the different aspects of the faces – eyebrows, mouth etc.

6. Ask the children to choose an emotion and then create the face that goes with this using the paper plates.

7. Create a display of faces, some which the children have made, others which you have photographed and some collected from magazines or newspapers.

KS2

1. Divide the class into groups.

2. Give each group a feelings dice.

3. Ask the groups to take turns in throwing the dice and then building a story around the emotion that they throw. For example:

    Sad – Max was really sad, he had lost his special toy dog.
    Angry – His brother kept calling him a cry baby, this made him very angry. His brother wouldn't stop so he chased after him.

4. Ask the children to write down their story in their groups and then share what they have come up with.

KS3

1. Watch the Mr Bean sandwich YouTube clip and discuss the different faces that Rowan Atkinson is able to make.

2. Ask the children to work in small groups. Ask each group to choose 6 emotions – no emotions can be the same. Then ask them to create the faces that show these emotions and photograph them.

3. Stick these different emotions on a dice and then play the Feelings Story Game.

4. Ask the groups to write down their story and then share what they came up with.

RESOURCES

1. Mr Bean 'Sandwich for Lunch' video: www.youtube.com/watch?v=jtqpuYvOfHY

2. Communication areas diagram

3. Communication percentages diagram

4. Facial expressions dice

5. Blank dice net

6. *The Saddest King* by Christopher Wormell

7. Paper plates

8. Wool

9. Coloured paper

10. Pens and crayons

11. Glue and sticky tape

IMPORTANT POINTS

Facial expressions support our understanding of others.

Facial expressions communicate how we are feeling to others.

LEARNING LINKS

Social and emotional competencies, co-operation, working together, communication with others, emotional literacy.

REFLECTION

Questions:

Positive comment from child:

Positive comment from adult:

LEARNING DIMENSIONS		SOCIAL & EMOTIONAL SKILLS	
Strategic awareness	🟧	Emotional literacy	🟩
Learning relationships	🟩	Neuroscience	
Curiosity		Self-regulation	
Creativity		Self-development	🟩
Meaning making			
Changing & learning			
Resilience			

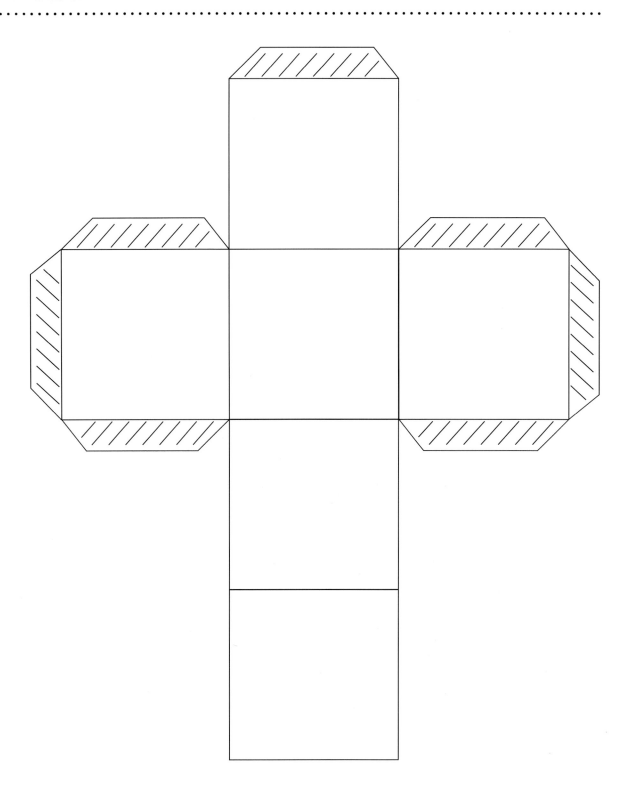

The language we use

SESSION OBJECTIVES

To understand that the language we use is only part of what we communicate to others.

To understand that the language we use can be very powerful.

SESSION OUTCOMES

✓ To be able to use words to show a variety of ways of interacting – kind and thoughtful, harsh and unkind, supportive and dismissive, motivating and passive.

LESSON PLAN

1. Share with the children a time when their class parent was supportive to their class baby – remind them of the words they used and the tone they were spoken in.

2. Explore types of words and tones of speech and what they can convey.

For those classrooms not able to undertake the Circles for Learning Project, video clips or photographs can be used to support the discussion around the topic and stimulate thoughts and ideas from the children and young people.

Task

KS1: To create a short play to show how words can be kind and thoughtful as well as unkind and hurtful.

KS2: To create a postcard that shares a positive message for a friend that they can read when they are down or sad.

KS3: To create a short radio play showing two different responses to a friend who is struggling, one which is thoughtful and kind one which is harsh and uncaring.

KS1

3.   Read the children *The Unkind Buffalo* by Jacquie Shepherd.

4.   Discuss the importance of words.

5.   Lay out a line on the floor and put numbers from 1–10 equally spaced along the line.

6.   Ask the children to stand on the line to show how they feel about the statement 'Words cannot hurt you', 1 being that they think this is not true and 10 believing that they think this is very true.

7.   Ask the children to think of an example when they have been hurt by words. Allow those who wish to share to do so. Remember a no name/blame culture is really important.

8.   Ask the children to put their hands up if they have ever used unkind words to anyone. Most will admit to this. Ask the adults to also share if they have done this.

9.   Ask the children to work in small groups and to create a short play to retell the story of 'The Unkind Buffalo', changing it to 'The Kind Buffalo'.

10.   Discuss the differences and why they happen.

KS2

1.   Read the children *Phileas's Fortune* by Agnes de Lestrade and Valeria Docampo.

2.   Discuss the importance of words.

3.   Lay out a line on the floor and put numbers from 1–10 equally spaced along the line.

4.   Ask the children to stand on the line to show how they feel about the statement 'Words are just words – they hold no power.'

5.   Ask each child to explain why they have stood where they have and to give an example to back up their belief.

6.   Share important speeches with the children – Martin Luther King, Winston Churchill, etc.

7.   Discuss how they make us feel.

8.   Share with the children some motivational or thoughtful phrases and ask them to choose one for a friend. Create a special postcard with the words on the card.

KS3

1. Lay out a line on the floor and put numbers from 1–10 equally spaced along the line.

2. Ask the children to stand on the line to show how they feel about the statement 'Words are just words – they hold no power.'

3. Ask each child to explain why they have stood where they have and to give an example to back up their belief.

4. Share important speeches with the children – Martin Luther King, Winston Churchill, etc.

5. Discuss how they make us feel.

6. Ask the young people to create two short radio plays showing an interaction between two friends. Play 1 has to show the interaction when one is using words badly, Play 2 shows what happens when they both try to use words wisely.

7. Come up with a phrase that promotes thinking about the words that we use to each other in the classroom.

RESOURCES

1. Examples of positive quotes

2. Examples of speeches that have motivated people

3. Paper and pens

4. 'The Unkind Buffalo' by Jacquie Shepherd

5. Dictionaries

6. Thesauruses

7. *Phileas's Fortune* by Agnes de Lestrade and Valeria Docampo

8. Motivational speech, www.youtube.com/watch?v=DjCLbtUOL3A

9. 'The 35 greatest speeches in history', www.artofmanliness.com/articles/the-35-greatest-speeches-in-history/

IMPORTANT POINTS

Language is a very powerful thing and can be used to support or destroy.

LEARNING LINKS

Social competencies, emotional literacy, speech and language, communication, working together, team work.

REFLECTION

Questions:

Positive comment from child:

Positive comment from adult:

LEARNING DIMENSIONS		SOCIAL & EMOTIONAL SKILLS	
Strategic awareness	🟧	Emotional literacy	
Learning relationships		Neuroscience	
Curiosity		Self-regulation	
Creativity	🟩	Self-development	🟩
Meaning making	🟧		
Changing & learning	🟩		
Resilience			

Thinking before you speak

SESSION OBJECTIVES

To enable children to understand that they need to think before they speak.

To support the understanding that thoughts are separate to speech.

SESSION OUTCOMES

✓ To create an acrostic poem on the topic of people thinking about their words so they do not hurt people.

✓ To design a hat that disposes of words if they are said to hurt people or are being used to be unkind.

✓ To create a cartoon strip to show why thinking before you speak is a positive strategy and can help avoid upsetting people.

LESSON PLAN

➢ Ask the children to describe a time when their class baby has been helped to understand how to say something. This might be a parent trying to get them to say 'please' or 'thank you' or to apologise.

➢ Discuss how the parent accomplished this. What strategies did they use? Why is this an important strategy to teach?

For those classrooms not able to undertake the Circles for Learning Project, video clips or photographs can be used to support the discussion around the topic and stimulate thoughts and ideas from the children and young people.

Task

KS1: To make an acrostic poem to show that we need to THINK before we speak.

KS2: To create a hat that can detect nasty or unkind words and dispose of them before they are said.

KS3: To create a cartoon character that is not able to filter what they say and the trouble this gets them into.

KS1

1. Share with the children a variety of acrostic poems and discuss how they are made.

2. Set the challenge that you want them to come up with an acrostic poem to help people think carefully about the words they use. It could be THINK, or it could be WORDS or another word that you all decide.

3. Discuss why words are important and that the words we use are our responsibility.

4. Work together to create example sentences, for example:

    Think about words carefully, they can bite and hurt
    Kind words make people smile inside

5. Share the poems together.

KS2

1. Share a clip about a factory getting rid of products that are defective.

2. Ask the children to design a hat that will dispose of words that are being used to hurt people or be unkind to people.

3. Share the 'Think before you speak' poster and look at the different skills needed. How will these be incorporated into the hat?

4. Discuss ideas and then ask children to work in pairs or individually to create their design.

5. Share the different designs and discuss how they operate.

6. Discuss the importance of everyone wearing an invisible hat that helps them use words wisely.

KS3

1. Read *The Word Collector* to the children and discuss Luna's character.

2. Ask the children to create a cartoon character that helps people use words wisely and kindly and then another character that does the opposite. Show one of these, or both, at work in a cartoon story strip.

3. Use the phrases in the book to support the children in thinking about the different settings that could be used. Magic words that caress the soul, words to fight hatred and violence, words to make the lonely and sad feel better or words to sooth those who are worried or anxious

4. Share together what the children create.

5. Discuss the concept about being thoughtful with the words we use and how they may be perceived.

RESOURCES

1. 'Filter what we say' poster

2. Examples of an acrostic poem

3. Examples of cartoon characters

4. Comic strip

5. Large paper

6. Pens

7. *The Word Collector* by Sonja Wimmer

IMPORTANT POINTS

Words are very powerful. They can hurt or they can make people feel good.

Because words are powerful we need to be careful how we use them. We are in control of the words and phrases we use.

LEARNING LINKS

Team work, social competencies, collaboration, friendships.

REFLECTION

Questions:

Positive comment from child:

Positive comment from adult:

LEARNING DIMENSIONS		SOCIAL & EMOTIONAL SKILLS	
Strategic awareness	🟧	Emotional literacy	🟩
Learning relationships	🟩	Neuroscience	
Curiosity		Self-regulation	
Creativity		Self-development	🟩
Meaning making			
Changing & learning			
Resilience			

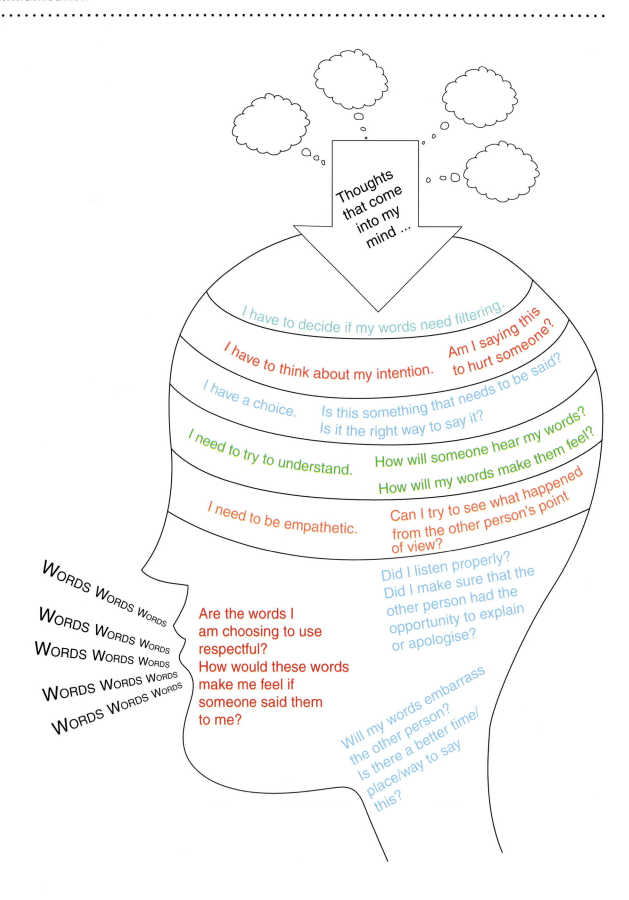

Thoughts that come into my mind …

I have to decide if my words need filtering.

I have to think about my intention.

Am I saying this to hurt someone?

I have a choice. Is this something that needs to be said? Is it the right way to say it?

I need to try to understand. How will someone hear my words? How will my words make them feel?

I need to be empathetic. Can I try to see what happened from the other person's point of view?

Did I listen properly? Did I make sure that the other person had the opportunity to explain or apologise?

Are the words I am choosing to use respectful? How would these words make me feel if someone said them to me?

Will my words embarrass the other person? Is there a better time/place/way to say this?

Words Words Words
Words Words Words
Words Words Words
Words Words Words
Words Words Words

COMIC STRIP

Conversational skills

SESSION OBJECTIVES

To be able to approach and start a conversation with a known person.

To be able to talk to a known person for 3 minutes and use a variety of open-ended questions to keep a conversation going.

SESSION OUTCOMES

✓ To be able to use a variety of questions to start a conversation with another child.

✓ To be able to use a variety of open questions to enable a conversation to run for several minutes.

LESSON PLAN

➤ Discuss with the children what their class baby does to engage with them.

➤ Explore the different strategies that their baby uses to get attention and then interact with them. Why is this skill important?

For those classrooms not able to undertake the Circles for Learning Project, video clips or photographs can be used to support the discussion around the topic and stimulate thoughts and ideas from the children and young people.

Task

KS1: To act out a variety of questions that could help start a conversation with someone new.

KS2/KS3: To be able to use a variety of open-ended questions to engage another person in a conversation.

KS1

1. Read the story of *Scaredy Squirrel Makes a Friend* by Melanie Watt

2. Discuss what it is like to make a new friend.

3.   Ask the children to draw themselves talking to a new person. Ask them to put 3 thinking bubbles over their head and the new person's head.

4.   What are some of the thoughts that are in your head? Share and think about the self-talk: 'They might not like me', 'They might not like the game I am suggesting', 'They may think I'm stupid.'

5.   Ask the children to draw in the thoughts above their head.

6.   What might the new person be thinking? 'What happens if they don't ask me to play?' 'What will I do if nobody talks to me?' 'What happens if nobody likes me, will I have to leave the school or play on my own all the time?'

7.   Ask the children to draw in the thoughts above the new person's head.

8.   Ask the children for good ideas about opening things they could say to a new person or someone they would like to be friends with.

9.   Make a list of the questions.

10. Discuss the pros and cons – try and help the children understand that the best questions are ones where the person has to say a bit and not just yes or no.

11. Play out some questions. If you use closed questions, get the children to give you a thumbs down and a negative buzzer noise.

KS2/KS3
1.   Ask the children to define 'conversation'.

2.   Divide the children into pairs and ask them to demonstrate a conversation.

3.   Ask what a good conversation is and a bad conversation.

4.   Choose examples from the children to demonstrate good conversations – open- ended questions, good listening, and positive body language.

5.   Help the children focus on types of questions – open ones that mean the person has to talk more and closed ones need a yes or no answer.

6.   Ask the children to imagine they are playing conversational tennis with their partner – can they go back and forwards 3 times each?

7.   Share some of the successful conversations and show how the questions link and build on each other.

HIT
Did you go on holiday this year?

OR

What was the best bit of your holiday this year?

ANSWER

I loved going snorkelling in the sea – that was the best bit.

RETURN

That sounds really exciting. Tell me about the things that you got to see.

ANSWER

Well, my favourite thing was watching the little fishes hide in the coral. When the bigger fishes swam past, they would quickly dive for cover and then peep out to see if the bigger fish had gone.

RETURN

That must have been really funny to watch, but tell me, how did it feel holding your breath under water and trying to see all the fishes?

ANSWER

It was really difficult to start with as every once in a while when you swam to the surface to take a breath, the water kept going down the snorkel and making me cough.

RETURN

How did you get over that?

8. Record who manages the longest rally without a yes or no answer.

9. Set the children a challenge – ask them to go home and test out their skill and see how many returns they can get.

RESOURCES

1. *Scaredy Squirrel Makes a Friend* by Melanie Watt

2. Paper

3. Pens

IMPORTANT POINTS

Body language and open-ended questions are important when initiating conversations.

Active listening is a useful skill when having a conversation with a person.

LEARNING LINKS

Working together, making friends, social competencies.

REFLECTION

Questions:

Positive comment from child:

Positive comment from adult:

LEARNING DIMENSIONS		SOCIAL & EMOTIONAL SKILLS	
Strategic awareness		Emotional literacy	🟩
Learning relationships	🟩	Neuroscience	
Curiosity		Self-regulation	
Creativity		Self-development	🟩
Meaning making			
Changing & learning	🟧		
Resilience			

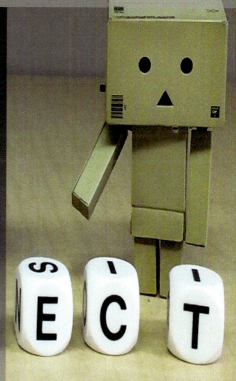

Chapter 2
Respecting yourself and others

CO-OPERATION   39

SHARING AND TAKING TURNS   42

NO BULLYING, TEASING OR
PUT-DOWNS   45

APPRECIATE THE BENEFITS
OF DIVERSITY AND CELEBRATE
DIFFERENCE   51

TREATING PEOPLE EQUALLY   55

BEING ASSERTIVE   59

EMPATHY: WALKING IN
ANOTHER PERSON'S SHOES   65

Co-operation

SESSION OBJECTIVES

To work together to achieve a task.

SESSION OUTCOMES

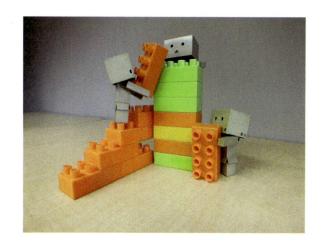

✓ To be able to guide another person through an obstacle course.

✓ To co-operate and achieve a given task.

LESSON PLAN

➢ Ask the children to remember a time when their class parent helped their class baby to achieve something.

➢ Explore how their class baby felt and why. This may involve trust – belief that has been developed through all the times they have been together.

For those classrooms not able to undertake the Circles for Learning Project, video clips or photographs can be used to support the discussion around the topic and stimulate thoughts and ideas from the children and young people.

Task

KS1/KS2/KS3: To guide their partner through an obstacle course.

KS1/KS2

1. Introduce the word co-operation.

2. Discuss what the children think it means, asking them to give examples of a time when they have seen this or experienced it.

3. Share the behaviours someone has to exhibit if you work with them. These may include honesty, kindness, thoughtfulness etc.

4. Focus on the word 'trust' when it is given as an example.

5. Explore this word together.

6. Pair up the children and explain that they are explorers who are lost in the jungle. One of them is blind due to an accident and the other is helping them negotiate the path so that they can get back to their camp.

7. Ask for one of each pair to go with you into the hall/field where you set up a jungle obstacle course. Label the obstacles with things you might find in the jungle – swamp, deadly snake etc.

8. Ask each pair you have been working with to go and get their partner. Blindfold their partners and then help them come to the hall/field.

9. Explain that their partner will talk them through the jungle path to safety. They are not allowed to touch them but can only use their voice and instructions.

10. Set off partners from different places so that more than one pair at a time can work.

11. Share what it was like for both partners before changing over.

12. Discuss how it felt and what strategies the lead used that helped the blindfolded child.

13. What made working together easy? What made it hard? Can they come up with their Top 10 skills for working with others?

KS3

1. Discuss the word co-operation and what the children feel it means. Ask them to give examples.

2. Share what makes co-operation easy and what makes it hard.

3. Ask the young people to work in pairs.

4. Give each pair a selection of equipment.

5. Ask each pair to work with another pair (making groups of 4).

6. One pair is to design an obstacle course for the other pair to negotiate. One of the pair to negotiate the course will be blindfolded.

7. Once one pair have tried the course then they create a different course for the other pair.

8. When both pairs have undertaken the course, the group can discuss what it was like. What made co-operation easy? What made it hard? Can they come up with their Top 10 skills for working with others and create a poster to share with others?

9. What is one skill they want to get better at and one skill that they want to introduce to their skill set that they don't normally use?

10. Share the two new skills with a partner – their partner's role is to ask each week how these new skills are growing.

RESOURCES

1. Equipment – skipping ropes, chairs, benches, cones, etc.

2. Blindfolds

IMPORTANT POINTS

Co-operating is an important skill in working with others. It can be learnt and a variety of skills can support this way of working. Listening, thinking about how someone else may feel, being flexible etc.

LEARNING LINKS

Social competencies, emotional literacy, working with others, communication.

REFLECTION

Questions:

Positive comment from child:

Positive comment from adult:

LEARNING DIMENSIONS		SOCIAL & EMOTIONAL SKILLS	
Strategic awareness		Emotional literacy	🟧
Learning relationships	🟩	Neuroscience	
Curiosity		Self-regulation	
Creativity		Self-development	🟩
Meaning making			
Changing & learning	🟩		
Resilience			

Sharing and taking turns

SESSION OBJECTIVES

To be able to understand the importance of taking turns.

To understand the importance of sharing.

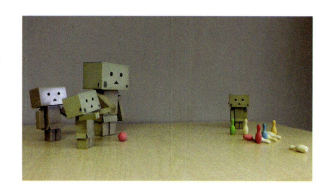

SESSION OUTCOMES

✓ To be able to explain why taking turns is a good skill to develop.

✓ To be able to explain why sharing is important.

LESSON PLAN

➢ Ask the children to share a time when they watched their baby learning how to take turns.

➢ Discuss how this skill is taught and why it is important for parents to teach to babies.

For those classrooms not able to undertake the Circles for Learning Project, video clips or photographs can be used to support the discussion around the topic and stimulate thoughts and ideas from the children and young people.

Task

KS1: To be able to play a game with a small group of others and take turns.

KS2: To be able to discuss how they would help a baby learn to share with others and why it is an important skill to learn.

KS1

1. Show the children a game of snakes and ladders. Ask them to describe how to play the game and what the rules are.

2. When a child talks about taking turns – explore this concept. How hard is it? How do we learn to do it? How can we support younger children learn the skill?

3. Where else is it important to take turns – make a list together.

4. Enjoy an afternoon of different games – all of which need children to take turns.

KS2

1. Ask the children to work in pairs and to discuss and make a list of different places where taking turns is important.

2. Share and create a collective list.

3. Ask the children how they learnt to take turns.

4. Working in pairs, ask the children to come up with two different ways that they could teach a younger child to take turns. This can be in any of the different ways they have identified.

5. Ask the children to bring a game into school that uses turn taking – then have a great afternoon sharing different games and practising taking turns.

RESOURCES

1. A variety of games to play where children have to take turns

2. Paper

3. Pens

IMPORTANT POINTS

Learning how to share and how to take turns are important social skills to have.

Sharing is not always easy and can make us feel a range of emotions.

LEARNING LINKS

Social competencies, working together, social skills, friendships, working relationships, team work.

REFLECTION

Questions:

Positive comment from child:

Positive comment from adult:

LEARNING DIMENSIONS		SOCIAL & EMOTIONAL SKILLS	
Strategic awareness	🟧	Emotional literacy	
Learning relationships		Neuroscience	
Curiosity		Self-regulation	
Creativity	🟩	Self-development	🟩
Meaning making	🟧		
Changing & learning	🟩		
Resilience			

No bullying, teasing or put-downs

SESSION OBJECTIVES

To explore and discuss the power of put-downs and unkind words or behaviours.

To explore how to manage if children are bullied.

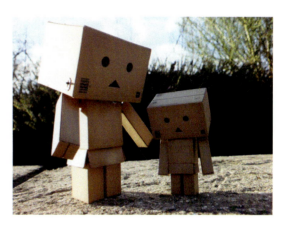

SESSION OUTCOMES

✓ To be able to show how being unkind with words or actions can make people feel.

✓ To create a Warm Fuzzy tree.

✓ To be able to discuss the bystander effect.

✓ To be able to create a short video to share with younger children on how to cope if they see someone being bullied.

LESSON PLAN

1. Ask the children to imagine their class baby's first day at school. How would they hope it goes? Can they describe how they would like their class baby to be treated?

2. How would they feel if their heard that on their first day another child had been unkind to them and made them cry?

For those classrooms not able to undertake the Circles for Learning Project, video clips or photographs can be used to support the discussion around the topic and stimulate thoughts and ideas from the children and young people.

Task

KS1: Act out a story about being bullied and then explore the different feelings of the characters involved.

KS2: Create a poster to show the different ways that bullying can be challenged.

KS3: To be able to discuss the bystander effect and what it means.

KS1

3. Read the story *Two* by Kathryn Otoshi.

4. Ask the children to divide into small groups and act out the story.

5. Explore how 2 felt when 1 went off with 3.

6. Explore how 2 felt when they heard 3 being unkind to 1.

7. Introduce the concept of bullying – being unkind again and again and again. Help the children understand that bullying is horrible as it is something that keeps happening.

8. Discuss what the other numbers did. How could they have helped rather than made things worse?

9. Introduce the concept of a Warm Fuzzy – something someone does that makes you feel warm and fuzzy inside. Ask the children to create a Warm Fuzzy which they can give someone if they do something kind or that makes them feel good. Create a Warm Fuzzy tree in the classroom to hang these on. It is useful to do this at the end of each day as part of a closing ritual for children. Teachers and other adults can join in.

KS2

1. Read the story *Nobody* by Erin Frankel to the children and explore how Thomas was made to feel by Kyle. What did he start believing?

2. Read *Nobody Knew What To Do* by Becky Ray McCain and discuss how the other children felt when they watched Ray being picked on. Why didn't they do something? What were they frightened off?

3. Discuss the meaning of bullying and come up with different ways that people who watched the bullying could do something. It is important to help children understand that they need to keep themselves safe so it is not always appropriate for them to stand up to a bully sometimes they need to find help in another way.

4. Ask the children to make a poster to show the different ways that bullying can be challenged or create an anti-bullying sign.

5. Introduce the concept of a Warm Fuzzy – something someone does that makes you feel warm and fuzzy inside. Ask the children to create a Warm Fuzzy which they can give someone if they do something kind or that makes them feel good. Create a Warm Fuzzy tree in the classroom to hang these on. It is useful to do this at the end of each day as part of a closing ritual for children. Teachers and other adults can join in.

KS3

1. Share a poem about bullying with the children.

2. Divide the class into groups of 3. Ask 1 person in each group to represent the bully, another to be the witness and the third to be the bully. Ask them to interview each other to explore how each person felt.

3. Discuss how the person being bullied might feel.

4. Discuss how the people witnessing the bullying felt.

5. Discuss how the bully felt.

6. Share the YouTube clip about the bystander effect.

7. Now they know of this, how do they feel?

8. How does knowing about this impact on their behaviour? What could they do if they witnessed someone being bullied in the future?

RESOURCES

1. 'The bystander effect' YouTube clip www.youtube.com/watch?v=Wy6eUTLzcU4

2. *Two* by Kathryn Otoshi

3. *Nobody* by Erin Frankel

4. *Nobody Knew What to Do* by Becky Ray McCain

5. Poems about bullying: 'Should've, Could've, Would've', by Emily Greenlee; 'Words Hurt' by Kaylynn (which can be found on the Internet)

6. Warm Fuzzy creature

IMPORTANT POINTS

Bullying has a huge impact on people.

Everyone has a responsibility to support others in some way. We can do this in many different ways.

We all have a responsibility to keep ourselves safe.

LEARNING LINKS

Social competencies, emotional literacy, working together.

REFLECTION

Questions:

Positive comment from child:

Positive comment from adult:

LEARNING DIMENSIONS		SOCIAL & EMOTIONAL SKILLS	
Strategic awareness	🟧	Emotional literacy	
Learning relationships		Neuroscience	
Curiosity		Self-regulation	
Creativity	🟩	Self-development	🟩
Meaning making	🟧		
Changing & learning	🟩		
Resilience			

Warm Fuzzies

Circles for Learning

Appreciate the benefits of diversity and celebrate difference

SESSION OBJECTIVES

To understand that we are all unique and special individuals.

SESSION OUTCOMES

✓ To be able to explain why differences are important and make the environment a more interesting and exciting place.

LESSON PLAN

➢ Ask the children to describe their class baby and what is special about them.

➢ Ask them to describe what they do or how they behave or look that makes them unique.

➢ Ask the children how a baby learns about the world that they live in – ask them to give an example. Focus on things that babies have learnt from their families – being frightened of spiders, enjoying books etc.

For those classrooms not able to undertake the Circles for Learning Project, video clips or photographs can be used to support the discussion around the topic and stimulate thoughts and ideas from the children and young people.

Task

KS1: To be able to create a picture to show why differences are important and make the environment a more interesting place.

KS2/KS3: To create a piece of art entitled 'Celebrating Difference'.

KS1/KS2

1. Show the children a bag of jelly babies all the same colour and a bag of normal mixed coloured ones.

2. Ask the question 'Would the manufacturers sell more of these or the mixed ones?'

3. Explore their answers. Pick up on the points about the mixed ones being better as there are lots of different tastes and flavours; you get bored with one flavour.

4. Share a picture of a flower bed where all the flowers are the same and then the flowers in a cottage garden and explore which is more exciting.

5. Link the observations the children have made to their class. What would it be like if there was a class of 30 children exactly alike?

6. Explore the pros and cons of a class of 30 children all exactly the same.

7. Share a picture of a crowd of people that shows diversity – help the children make the link about this being more exciting but also having difficulties depending on people's knowledge and beliefs.

8. Ask the children to create a picture to show why differences are important and make the environment a more exciting place. They could use a split screen effect to demonstrate this if they wanted.

KS3

1. Show the children a bag of jelly babies all the same colour and a bag of normal mixed coloured ones.

2. Ask the question 'Would the manufacturers sell more of these or the mixed ones?'

3. Explore their answers. Pick up on the points about the mixed ones being better as there are lots of different tastes and flavours; you get bored with one flavour.

4. Share a picture of a flower bed where all the flowers are the same and then the flowers in a cottage garden and explore which is more exciting.

5. Link the observations the children have made to their class. What would it be like if there was a class of 30 children exactly alike?

6. Explore the pros and cons of a class of 30 children all exactly the same.

7. Share a picture of a crowd of people that shows diversity – help the children make the link about this being more exciting but also having difficulties depending on people's knowledge and beliefs.

8. Discuss where people's knowledge and beliefs come from. Are they always correct? How do you know if your beliefs are correct or not?

9. Create a piece of art work entitled 'Celebrating Difference'.

RESOURCES

1. 1 bag of jelly babies all the same colour

2. 1 bag of mixed jelly babies

3. A picture of flowers in a border all exactly the same

4. A picture of a country cottage border full of lots of different flowers

5. A picture of a large group of people from many different cultures and backgrounds.

6. Selection of art materials

IMPORTANT POINTS

Diversity is exciting and brings great interest. We are all unique individuals and that is very special and important.

LEARNING LINKS

Working together, friendships, emotional literacy, speaking and listening, thinking skills.

REFLECTION

Questions:

Positive comment from child:

Positive comment from adult:

LEARNING DIMENSIONS		SOCIAL & EMOTIONAL SKILLS	
Strategic awareness	🟧	Emotional literacy	
Learning relationships		Neuroscience	
Curiosity		Self-regulation	
Creativity	🟩	Self-development	🟩
Meaning making	🟧		
Changing & learning	🟩		
Resilience			

Treating people equally

SESSION OBJECTIVES

To explore what treating people equally is and whether this is enough.

SESSION OUTCOMES

✓ To enable children to understand what it means to be discriminated against.

✓ To enable children to explore the concept of equality.

✓ To be able to recognise discriminatory behaviour.

✓ To understand that some people are treated unfairly because of their characteristics.

LESSON PLAN

➢ Explore with the children how their class baby learns to behave and how they learn what to believe.

➢ What would they like for their class baby to be like?

➢ How could they ensure that this happens as a parent?

For those classrooms not able to undertake the Circles for Learning Project, video clips or photographs can be used to support the discussion around the topic and stimulate thoughts and ideas from the children and young people.

Task

KS1: To read and discuss the book *Strictly No Elephants* by Lisa Mantchev.

KS2/KS3: To understand and be able to describe what being discriminated against means.
To be able to create a poster to show what discrimination looks like and what should happen to make things equal.

KS1

1. Read the story *Strictly No Elephants* and discuss.

2. Why did the Pet Club make a sign, Strictly No Elephants? How did that make the boy and his elephant feel? Why did he choose to make a club of his own? Which club would have been the most interesting and why?

3. Explore why some people shut out others. Introduce the word discrimination and discuss if this is OK.

4. What sort of sign would they like on their class door?

5. How can they, as a class, make sure that everyone is treated equally?

KS2/KS3

1. As the children enter the class, ask those with brown eyes to come and sit at the front and those with blue eyes to stand behind them.

2. Wait for one child to verbalise that this isn't fair and then ask them to explain what they mean. Why should people be treated equally?

3. Explore why people may be discriminated against – age, gender, disability, religion etc.

4. Ask the children to come up with the words for each group – racism, ageism, sexism, homophobia, transphobia, discriminated against on the grounds of disability, religion and beliefs, and pregnancy and maternity.

5. Ask the children to sit in small groups/tables. Share the paper with the different words on and ask them as a group to give an example and then pass the paper on. All groups need to give an example for each category.

6. Share what they have found.

7. Remind them of how it felt when they were discriminated against.

8. Share with the children the Equality and Justice picture and discuss in groups.

9. Ask the children to create a picture either on their own or in pairs that shows what discrimination is and what they would like instead.

RESOURCES

1. A range of discriminating photographs

2. *Strictly No Elephants* by Lisa Mantchev

3. Paper

4.   Pens

5.   Equality and Justice picture from the Internet

IMPORTANT POINTS

Discrimination is not acceptable and everyone has the right to equality.

LEARNING LINKS

Working together, social competencies, friendship, emotional literacy, development of self, challenging beliefs, equality.

REFLECTION

Questions:

Positive comment from child:

Positive comment from adult:

LEARNING DIMENSIONS		SOCIAL & EMOTIONAL SKILLS	
Strategic awareness	🟧	Emotional literacy	
Learning relationships		Neuroscience	
Curiosity		Self-regulation	
Creativity	🟩	Self-development	🟩
Meaning making	🟧		
Changing & learning	🟩		
Resilience			

Racism	Sexism
Ageism	Homophobia
Transphobia	Anti-Semitism
Classism	Ableism
Sizeism	Colourism
Lookism	Nativism
Cisism/cissexism	Ethnocentrism
Intellectualism	Speciesism

Being assertive

SESSION OBJECTIVES

To understand the difference between passive, assertive and aggressive.

To be able to demonstrate being assertive, explaining how you feel, what you want and being flexible.

SESSION OUTCOME

✓ To be able to explain the difference between being passive, assertive, aggressive and passive aggressive.

✓ To be able to demonstrate being aggressive, being passive and being assertive.

LESSON PLAN

➢ Ask the children to describe their class baby. Explore how the baby has learnt to behave in these ways.

➢ Explore as a parent 3 ways you would want your child to behave and then how you would teach them these behaviours.

For those classrooms not able to undertake the Circles for Learning Project, video clips or photographs can be used to support the discussion around the topic and stimulate thoughts and ideas from the children and young people.

Task

KS1: To create a puppet play to show passive, aggressive and assertive behaviour.

KS2: To be able to describe the difference between passive, aggressive, passive aggressive and assertive behaviours.
To be able to create puppet play for younger children helping them understand the differences between the different ways of behaving and communicating.

KS3: To be able to create a short video showing the differences in the different types of behaviour.

Respecting yourself and others

KS1

1. Using puppets, act out a situation where one puppet wants to do something and the other is not really keen but goes along with it – passive. Help the children understand that this means that the puppet's wishes are being 'passed over'.

2. Explore why someone might behave in that way. They might feel that if they didn't they would lose their friends, they don't want to cause a fuss, they don't think their views are important, they just want to keep the peace.

3. Ask the children how the puppets might behave if one puppet was aggressive – let the children explore the two concepts and show their different puppet plays.

4. Discuss how it feels when someone is aggressive.

5. Introduce the concept of being assertive – this is where someone is able to say

    ✓ How they feel – I feel really fed up when you don't listen to me.

    ✓ Why – It makes me think that you are not interested in what I have to say.

    ✓ What they would like – make a suggestion about what should happen – it would be so much better if you could let me finish what I have to say, without interrupting me and then consider what I am suggesting.

6. Ask the children to create a short puppet play to show this in action.

7. Share and discuss.

KS2

1. Explore with the children the words 'aggressive', 'passive aggressive' and 'assertive'.

2. Ask the children to work in small groups – pass the words around and ask them to give an example, write a definition or write why someone might behave in this way on the sheet.

3. Explore what the children have come up with and discuss the different meanings.

4. Ask the children to work in groups and show what one of these concepts might look like using puppets. Explain that you want to use each of the puppet shows put together to help one of the younger classes understand the difference so that they can practise being assertive.

5. Pull out good examples and share with the class and then discuss how it makes them feel, if they have experienced this and what it might be like from both points of view.

6. Agree on a definition for each word.

7. Share the puppet show with another class.

KS3

1. Introduce the words 'aggressive', 'passive aggressive' and 'assertive' – discuss what they mean.

2. Share the video clip and ask the young people to say which clip is portraying which behaviour. Discuss how the different people feel in each clip.

3. Introduce the phrase 'passive aggressive' – watch the video clip to help understand this.

4. Discuss each of the behaviours and ask which one is the most useful to know about, promote and become confident with.

5. Ask the children to create a short video clip to show to younger children the difference in the behaviours and how to be assertive.

6. Share and discuss the different videos.

RESOURCES

1. Puppets

2. Paper

3. Pens

4. Assertive statement cards

5. Word definition cards

6. Word cards

7. 'Being assertive' YouTube clip by the Samaritans: www.youtube.com/watch?v=n-IfXVpliUI

8. 'The ten most passive aggressive phrases' YouTube clip www.youtube.com/watch?v=1Cr1ztMqdro

IMPORTANT POINTS

Understanding that we have the ability to choose which way we respond and that being assertive allows our needs and thoughts to be heard and understood without hurting or frightening others.

LEARNING LINKS

Working together, friendships, emotional literacy, social competencies, collaboration.

REFLECTION

Questions:

Positive comment from child:

Positive comment from adult:

LEARNING DIMENSIONS		SOCIAL & EMOTIONAL SKILLS	
Strategic awareness	🟧	Emotional literacy	
Learning relationships		Neuroscience	
Curiosity		Self-regulation	
Creativity	🟩	Self-development	🟩
Meaning making	🟧		
Changing & learning	🟩		
Resilience			

Assertive

Passive

Aggressive

Passive Aggressive

Sarah walks into her Geography lesson late for the third time that week and explains that her Mum's car broke down. Her Geography teacher does not believe her.	Bobby has been invited to his friend's birthday party but his parents want him to look after his little sister that night and don't want him to go.
Robert has forgotten to bring his football team shirt to school and his teacher doesn't believe that it is at his Dad's house where he left it after the game last week. He believes that Robert has forgotten it.	Nita and Sharn are waiting for lunch in the dining hall. The lunch line is very slow as one of the serving ladies is off sick. They have to turn up to their netball practice and if they are late then they won't be in the team.
Tye and Sean are in the art room working. When the art teacher comes in she notices that one of the children's pots has been broken. She immediately blames the boys for mucking around in the art room and breaking it.	Priti and Sasha have been working on a costume for the school production. They are both part of the costumes team. The costume has gone missing. The Drama teacher blames them for losing it as they were the last people to see it.
Nim has just come in to the changing room from the football field. The Coach comes in and sees mud all over the floor. The Coach gets cross with Nim for making such a mess and puts him in detention.	Tara has just got home from school; the house is empty. She goes to her room and listens to music. When her Mum comes in she blames Tara for all the washing up in the sink and grounds her for the weekend.

Passive

Accepting or allowing what happens or what others do, without active response or resistance.

Aggressive

Ready or likely to attack or confront in a determined and forceful way.

Passive Aggressive

A type of behaviour characterized by indirect resistance to the demands of others and an avoidance of direct confrontation, often with the use of so-called humour.

Assertive

The quality of being self-assured and confident without being aggressive. It enables a person to say what they feel, what they would like and also be flexible in negotiating this.

Empathy: Walking in another person's shoes

SESSION OBJECTIVES

To look at a situation from another person's point of view.

To be able to show that another person's feelings and needs can be thought about or considered.

SESSION OUTCOMES

✓ To work in groups to discuss and then put thoughts and feelings onto empathy pictures.

✓ To be able to describe what empathy is to a partner.

LESSON PLAN

➢ Ask the children to share a time when they watched their class parent know what their class baby wanted/needed despite the fact that their class baby wasn't able to tell them.

➢ Explore the concept together of knowing what someone else is feeling and why.

For those classrooms not able to undertake the Circles for Learning Project, video clips or photographs can be used to support the discussion around the topic and stimulate thoughts and ideas from the children and young people.

Task

KS1: To read the book *Stand in My Shoes* by Bob Sornson and discuss what it is like for someone else.

KS2: To be able to show through discussion what it is like for another person and what could be done to support them.

Respecting yourself and others

KS3: To be able to show through discussion how someone else might be feeling, why and what could be done to help them.

KS1

1. Read the book *Stand in My Shoes* and discuss the word 'empathy' and how someone else might be feeling.

2. Read the story of 'Goldilocks and the Three Bears'.

3. Ask the children to stand in the shoes (have a variety of shoes to use that represent the three bears and Goldilocks) of the different characters and say how they were feeling.

   - Goldilocks when she went into the three bears' home
   - Goldilocks when she started eating Baby Bear's porridge
   - Daddy Bear when he got home and found his home had been broken into
   - Mummy Bear when she realised her porridge had been eaten
   - Baby Bear when he realised his chair had been broken
   - Each of the bears when they realised someone was still in their house
   - Goldilocks when she woke up to find the three bears looking at her.

KS2

1. Read the book *Stand in My Shoes* and discuss the word 'empathy' and how someone else might be feeling.

2. Ask the children to work in groups and then share a selection of pictures with each group.

   - Ask the children to write in thinking bubbles what the different people might be thinking.
   - On in heart-shaped sticky notes, write what they might be feeling.
   - On square sticky notes write what needs to happen/what someone could do to help.

3. Ask each group to present their pictures and thoughts and ideas to the rest of the class.

4. Discuss what they came up with.

5. Share with the class 'Class Angels'. We each become a secret Class Angel for someone in the class (ensure everyone has one) as their Secret Angel. We watch for when they are down or sad or excited or frightened and do something about it. We have to do this in secret so they don't know who we are. If our partner was sad because they had lost their shoes we might encourage other people to help them look for them, or if they didn't have a partner we might offer for them to join our group or we might organise people to sign a birthday card for them or remind the teacher that it is their turn to go first in the queue.

KS3

1. Watch the YouTube clip on the empathy deficit.

2. Discuss what empathy is.

3. Ask the children to work in groups and then share a selection of pictures with each group.

   - Ask the children to write in thinking bubbles what the different people might be thinking.
   - On in heart-shaped sticky notes, write what they might be feeling.
   - On square sticky notes, write what needs to happen/what someone could do to help.

4. Ask each group to present their pictures and thoughts and ideas to the rest of the class.

5. Discuss what prevents us from doing things.

RESOURCES

1. 'Stand in my shoes: Exposing and erasing the empathy deficit', www.kickstarter.com/projects/peacelily/stand-in-my-shoes-exposing-and-erasing-the-empathy

2. Empathy pictures set

3. Heart-shaped sticky notes

4. Thinking bubbles sticky notes

5. Square sticky notes

IMPORTANT POINTS

To explore how another person might feel.

By thinking about other people we might want to change our behaviour.

LEARNING LINKS

Speaking and listening, collaboration, information processing, questioning, observation, creativity, planning and organisation, teamwork.

REFLECTION

Questions:

Positive comment from child:

Positive comment from adult:

LEARNING DIMENSIONS		SOCIAL & EMOTIONAL SKILLS	
Strategic awareness	🟧	Emotional literacy	
Learning relationships		Neuroscience	
Curiosity		Self-regulation	
Creativity	🟩	Self-development	🟩
Meaning making	🟧		
Changing & learning	🟩		
Resilience			

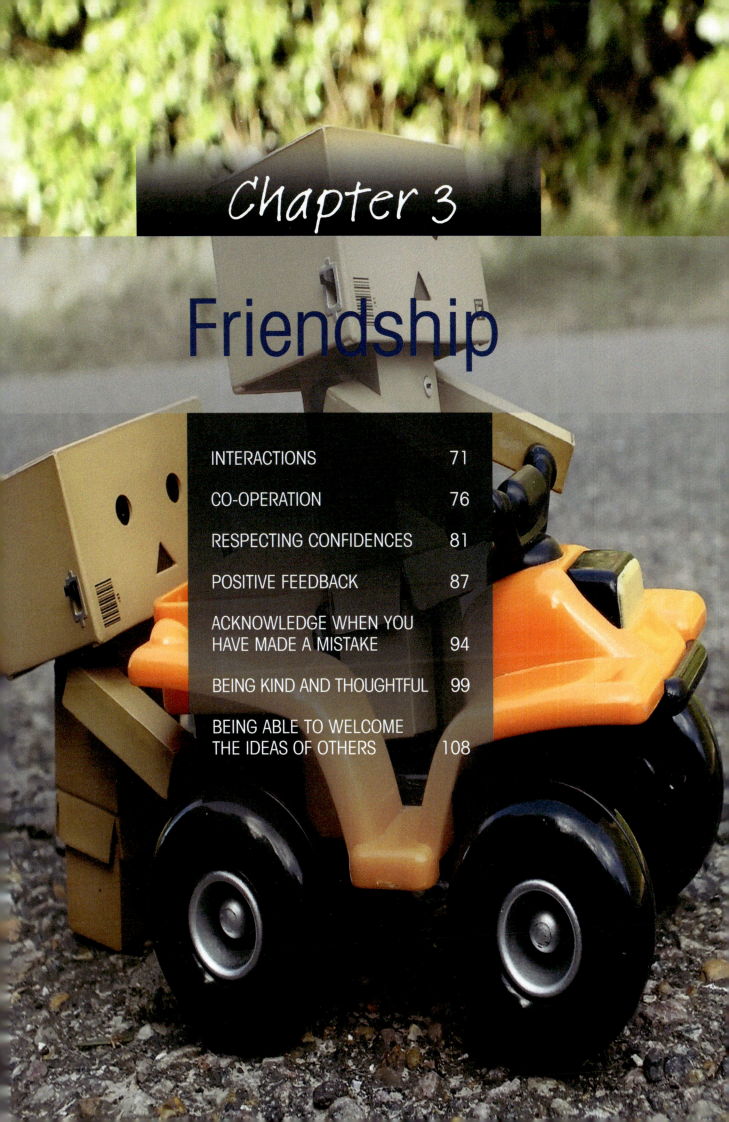

Chapter 3

Friendship

INTERACTIONS	71
CO-OPERATION	76
RESPECTING CONFIDENCES	81
POSITIVE FEEDBACK	87
ACKNOWLEDGE WHEN YOU HAVE MADE A MISTAKE	94
BEING KIND AND THOUGHTFUL	99
BEING ABLE TO WELCOME THE IDEAS OF OTHERS	108

Interactions

SESSION OBJECTIVES

To understand that how we behave and interact with others influences how we are seen.

To understand that positive social interactions support good relationships.

SESSION OUTCOMES

✓ To be able to share and describe what positive interactions are.

✓ To be able to identify positive interactions and explain how they support the relationships with others.

LESSON PLAN

➢ Ask the children to describe a time when they watched their class parent model positive interactions.

➢ Explore why this is influential for how their class baby will learn to behave.

For those classrooms not able to undertake the Circles for Learning Project, video clips or photographs can be used to support the discussion around the topic and stimulate thoughts and ideas from the children and young people.

Task

KS1: To be able to describe positive interactions. To create a class poster showing what positive interactions are.

KS2: To be able to describe what positive interactions are. To take photos of positive interactions and create a card game for younger children.

KS3: To video a small group of peers working together and to identify and share positive interactions that they are displaying.

KS1

1. In pairs ask the children to come up with 5 positive interactions.

2. Share and discuss in class. Explore what an interaction is and how they can be positive or negative. Discuss what happens if the person who initiates the interaction feels it is

positive but the other person feels it is negative – what might be a good way to manage this? Whose fault is it?

3. Give the children 10 of the top suggestions on slips of paper and ask them in their pairs to put them in order.

4. Ask the pairs to share their top 10 order and discuss why they decided upon them.

5. Share the top 10 interactions throughout the class, asking for each pair to draw a picture to illustrate their interaction. Give the children circles to draw their pictures in.

6. Join all the pictures together to make a class top 10 interactions poster.

KS2
1. Explore with the children what an interaction is. Use the chain links to show how one action leads to another and so on.

2. Ask the children to work in pairs and to come up with 5 positive and 5 negative interactions. Ask them to write them on the paper chains to show how one interaction leads to another.

3. Ask the children to share what they have found and discuss what they have learnt through looking at the interactions.

4. Pose the question – if a child acts with good intention but the receiver feels this is unkind – who is to blame? What should happen?

5. Ask the children to work in pairs and to come up with a game to help younger children understand about interactions and how they can be negative or positive and that one action leads to another and so has a consequence or an effect on how another person responds.

6. Share the games with another younger class and then share the feedback with the children.

KS3
1. Explore with the children what an interaction is. Use the chain links to show how one action leads to another and so on.

2. Ask the children to work in pairs and to come up with 5 positive and 5 negative interactions. Ask them to write them on the paper chains to show how one interaction leads to another.

3. Ask the children to share what they have found and discuss what they have learnt through looking at the interactions.

4. Pose the question – if a child acts with good intention but the receiver feels this is unkind – who is to blame? What should happen?

5. Ask the children to work in small groups of 4 and to undertake a team task – this might be to construct the tallest tower out of newspaper or to make a tower out of spaghetti and marshmallows or another such group challenge.

6. Put two groups together. Whilst group 1 undertakes the task, group 2 has to video the group interacting. It is useful to ask one child to video and then the others to watch the interactions and note positive ones – with an action and then the reaction. Once group 1 has completed their task, group 2 undertakes theirs with group 1 videoing.

7. When both groups have undertaken their videos, their job is to identify as many positive interactions as possible. They need to highlight the video clip and then describe the action that started the interaction and the reaction and also state why it was positive. Make sure the children focus on the positive interactions and do not highlight or talk about the ones that went wrong or were negative.

8. When the groups have prepared, they need to feed back to their partner group and show them the interactions and share why they felt they were positive.

9. Once all groups have fed back, discuss what they have learnt and how they felt the session had supported their understanding of interactions.

RESOURCES

1. Paper

2. Pens

3. Tablet computer

4. Large sheets of paper

5. Card

6. Glue

7. Paper chains

IMPORTANT POINTS

Positive interactions support relationships.

Positive interactions can be learnt, practised and then chosen to be used.

LEARNING LINKS

Social skills, friendships, emotional literacy, working together, collaboration.

REFLECTION

Questions:

Positive comment from child:

Positive comment from adult:

LEARNING DIMENSIONS		SOCIAL & EMOTIONAL SKILLS	
Strategic awareness		Emotional literacy	🟧
Learning relationships	🟩	Neuroscience	
Curiosity		Self-regulation	🟧
Creativity		Self-development	🟩
Meaning making			
Changing & learning			
Resilience			

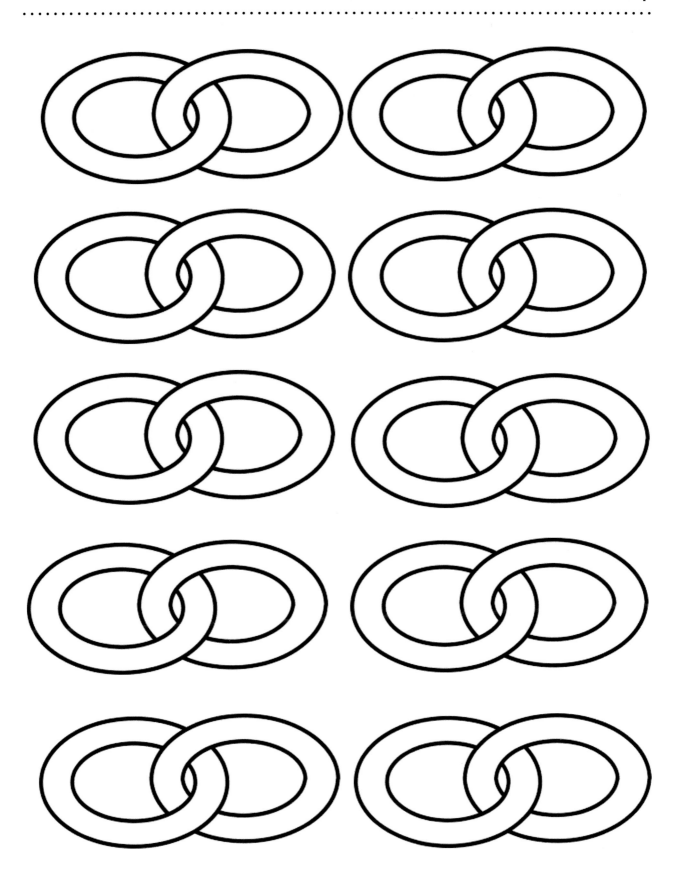

Co-operation

SESSION OBJECTIVES

To work as a group to achieve a set outcome.

To be able to share and discuss the skills needed to work successfully with others.

SESSION OUTCOMES

✓ To be able to work with others to achieve a set task.

✓ To be able to describe co-operative behaviours and attitudes.

LESSON PLAN

➤ Ask the children to share a time when they watched their parent and class baby work together to achieve a goal.

➤ Explore the skills that the parent used to support the class baby.

For those classrooms not able to undertake the Circles for Learning Project, video clips or photographs can be used to support the discussion around the topic and stimulate thoughts and ideas from the children and young people.

Task

KS1: To work in pairs and accomplish the Mad Relay.
KS2: To work with a partner to create a shared drawing.
KS3: To share with the group a game that develops co-operation.

KS1

1. Ask the children what co-operation means and to share an example.

2. Divide the class into 4 teams and find a large space where they can undertake a relay race together.

3. Explain to the teams that they need to work in pairs to get an object from one end of the course to the other.

4. Call each pair up to the start and ask them to pull out a card to show the way they need to work together. Ask then to transport a range of objects depending on the body parts they have to have touching. The objects could be a ball, skipping rope, bean bag, hoop, etc.

5. Let the children have a practice go so that they can learn to work together.

6. Whilst they practise, point out good collaboration and explain why it is working.

7. Now have fun!!

KS2

1. Ask the children to define co-operation and to give examples of when they have been involved in co-operation when it went well.

2. Discuss what enables co-operation to be positive – what skills and behaviours do they need to use? List these on the board.

3. Ask the children to work in pairs.

4. Give each pair a set of pens or coloured pencils and a piece of A3 paper/A5 paper.

5. Explain that they are to take turns to create a picture showing a children's story or fairy tale. They take it in turns to draw something in the picture until the picture is completed, e.g., if the children chose 'Goldilocks and the Three Bears', person 1 might draw the house of the three bears; then it is person 2's go. They might draw Goldilocks sitting at the table eating Baby Bear's porridge. It is person 1's turn again – they might draw Daddy Bear, Person 2 might then draw Mummy Bear – this continues until the picture is completed and tells the story.

6. Share the pictures and discuss how the children felt about the game – what was difficult? How did they feel when their partner drew something in a different way than how they had thought it should be drawn? What strategies did they use to work together?

KS3

1. Ask the children to define the word 'co-operation' and to give examples of when they have been involved in co-operating with others to achieve a task.

2. Discuss the skills needed.

3. Ask the groups to work in pairs and to research a game that demonstrates and practises co-operation.

4. Ask each pair to share the game that they have found with the class.

5. The pairs listening need to give the game a mark out of 10 for co-operation and enjoyment. Choose the top 3 games and ask the pairs who found them to teach the rest of the group how to play.

6. Discuss the games and choose the one that was most fun and also practised co-operation.

RESOURCES

1. A range of objects to use in the Mad Relay

2. Large paper

3. Pens

4. Access to the internet

IMPORTANT POINTS

Co-operation is important if a task is to be achieved.

Co-operation is made up of a variety of skills and behaviours.

LEARNING LINKS

Friendships, working together, collaboration, emotional literacy, social competencies.

REFLECTION

Questions:

Positive comment from child:

Positive comment from adult:

LEARNING DIMENSIONS		SOCIAL & EMOTIONAL SKILLS	
Strategic awareness	🟧	Emotional literacy	🟧
Learning relationships	🟩	Neuroscience	
Curiosity		Self-regulation	🟧
Creativity		Self-development	🟩
Meaning making			
Changing & learning			
Resilience			

Shoulder to shoulder	Back to back
Elbow to elbow	Forehead to forehead
Chin to chin	Knee to knee
Finger to finger	Palm to palm
Cheek to cheek	Hip to hip
Head to head	Hand to knee
Finger to elbow	Back to shoulder

Respecting confidences

SESSION OBJECTIVES

To understand that respecting confidences is important.

To understand that some confidences need to be shared with others.

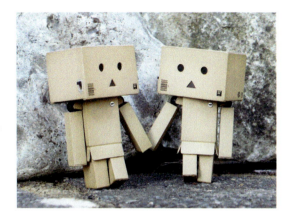

SESSION OUTCOMES

✓ To be able to understand why it is important to keep information a friend shares to themselves.

✓ To be able to share why some confidences would need to be shared with an adult.

✓ To be able to model how they would share with their friend that a confidence told to them is not safe and needs to be shared.

LESSON PLAN

1. Ask the children to think about their class baby's first day at school. What sort of day would they like this to be?

2. What sort of friend would they like their class baby to become, what skills and behaviours would they like them to demonstrate?

For those classrooms not able to undertake the Circles for Learning Project, video clips or photographs can be used to support the discussion around the topic and stimulate thoughts and ideas from the children and young people.

Task

KS1/KS2: To be able to share which things a friend might tell them that they need to keep private and which things they might say need to be shared with an adult.

KS3: To create a short sketch to show how they would explain to a friend that the information they had shared with them needs to be shared with an adult.

KS1/KS2

1. Discuss as a group what a confidence is and why it is special.

2. Think of confidences that friends might tell them – what they had bought for a friend's birthday, that they had stayed up late and read their book even when their Mum had told them to go to sleep, that they had eaten an extra cake that their Grandmother had made even though their Dad had said they couldn't have another one, etc.

3. Explore with the children what would happen if they broke the confidence of the person who had told them: If they told their friend what their other friend was giving them for their birthday – how would each person feel? Would they tell them a confidence again? Would their friend trust them in the future?

4. Ask the children to work in pairs and create a list of 5–10 things that a friend might tell them in confidence that would be important for them to keep to themselves.

5. OR give the children one of the stories and ask them to work in pairs to show how the different people would feel in the stories. They could share how people would feel by talking or draw pictures to show the different people and how they would feel. When they have done this, ask them to decide on the consequence of sharing the confidence.

6. Share the work as a class and discuss how the different people might feel and what the consequence of their actions would be.

7. Pose the question, is it always right to keep a confidence?

8. Set out a line in the classroom and ask the children to stand on the line – one end is 'Yes, it is always right to keep a confidence' and then other end is 'No, confidences should never be kept'. Ask them to stand on the line showing what they think.

9. Ask each person to give an example to support their position.

10. Ask the children to work in pairs and to answer the question, how do you decide whether it is right to keep the confidence or not?

11. Share and discuss.

KS3

1. Discuss as a group what a confidence is and why it is special.

2. Think of confidences that friends might tell them – what they had boought for a friend's birthday, that they had stayed up late and read their book even when their Mum had told them to go to sleep, that they hadn't done their homework as they had been talking to their boyfriend on the phone, that they had told their parents that they didn't have any homework as they wanted to go to their friends for a sleepover, etc.

3. Explore with the children what would happen if they broke the confidence of the person who had told them: if they told their friend what their other friend was giving them for their birthday – how would each person feel? Would they tell them a confidence again? Would their friend trust them in the future?

4. Pose the question, is it always right to keep a confidence?

5. Set out a line in the classroom and ask the children to stand on the line – one end is 'Yes, it is always right to keep a confidence' and the other end is 'No, confidences should never be kept'. Ask them to stand on the line showing what they think.

   Ask each person to give an example to support their position.

6. Ask the children to work in pairs and create a list of 10 things that a friend might tell them in confidence that would be important for them to keep to themselves and 10 things that would be dangerous/not right to keep secret.

7. Share the types of confidences that they have collected.

8. Ask the young people if they decided that it wasn't safe/right/OK to keep a confidence. How could they tell their friend?

9. Ask the young people to work in small groups and create a short sketch to show how they could do this in a thoughtful and considerate way.

10. Share the sketches and discuss.

RESOURCES

1. Paper

2. Pens

3. Tablet computer

4. Confidence stories

IMPORTANT POINTS

Information shared by a friend is important.

Information shared by a friend may need to be shared with an adult to keep their friend or another person safe.

LEARNING LINKS

Safeguarding, PSHE, friendships, relationships.

REFLECTION

Questions:

Positive comment from child:

Positive comment from adult:

LEARNING DIMENSIONS		SOCIAL & EMOTIONAL SKILLS	
Strategic awareness		Emotional literacy	🟩
Learning relationships	🟩	Neuroscience	
Curiosity		Self-regulation	
Creativity		Self-development	🟩
Meaning making			
Changing & learning			
Resilience			

Sally and Emma are good friends. Emma tells Sally that she has bought her Dad a special calendar with pictures of motorcycles on for his Christmas present. Sally tells Emma's Dad about the calendar Emma has brought for him.	**Dad**
	Emma
	Sally
	Consequence

Tom and Mark are good friends with Pete. It is Pete's birthday soon and Tom has planned to take him fishing. Mark tells Pete what Tom has planned.	**Tom**
	Mark
	Pete
	Consequence

Anita and Sharn are both good friends and live next door to each other. Anita tells Sharn that she sneaked downstairs and got her book and then stayed up late reading despite the fact that her Mum had told her not to and had taken the book downstairs.	**Mum**
	Sharn
	Anita
	Consequence

Tyrone Frasier and Nim were all friends and were all in the same class at school. Nim told them both on the way to school that his dog had thrown up over his coat but that his Mum hadn't had time to wash it properly. Tyrone told the other boys in the class who kept saying he smelt at playtime.	**Tyrone**
	Frasier
	Nim
	Consequence

Tim and Sally have been invited to Ella's birthday party. Ella asks them not to tell Felix about the party as he is not invited. Tim tells Felix that he is going to Ella's party and that he hasn't been invited.	**Felix**
	Tim
	Sally
	Ella
	Consequence

Mrs Bailey tells Sam and Gowri that she has a surprise for her class later that day as she has arranged for the fire engine and the firemen to come into school. Sam tells the children in her class about the surprise.	**Mrs Bailey**
	Sam
	Gowri
	Consequence

Freddie and Pattie are both in class with Sheva. Sheva tells them both that she has sneaked her special teddy into school even though her Mum told her she couldn't bring her to school. Freddie tells her Mum when she comes to pick her up after school.	**Freddie**
	Sheva
	Pattie
	Consequence

Biancca and Cindy are friends Cindy tells Biancca that she has got a surprise for their teacher Mrs Harris as she is leaving and that her Mum will bring in a bunch of flowers at the end of the day so she can give them to her. Biancca tells Mrs Harris about Cindy's surprise.	**Cindy**
	Mrs Harris
	Biancca
	Consequence

Tom and Harry are friends and live near a wood. Harry makes a special camp and tells Tom where it is but asks him not to tell anyone as he wants it to be his special place. Tom tells some of the other boys at school who go and find the camp.	**Tom**
	Harry
	Consequence

Steph, Barry and Tia are all friends. Tia tells Steph that she doesn't like Barry's new school bag. Steph tells Barry.	**Tia**
	Steph
	Barry
	Consequence

Positive feedback

SESSION OBJECTIVES

To be able to give positive feedback.

To be able to understand that both the words and how we say things create a message to another person.

SESSION OUTCOMES

✓ To be able to give positive feedback to a peer.

✓ To be able to use a variety of language and tone to ensure that positive feedback is given.

LESSON PLAN

1. Ask the children to remember a time when their class parent was helping their class baby achieve something. What skills and behaviours did they use?

2. What was the outcome of their behaviour?

For those classrooms not able to undertake the Circles for Learning Project, video clips or photographs can be used to support the discussion around the topic and stimulate thoughts and ideas from the children and young people.

Task

KS1: To be able to demonstrate using puppets to give positive feedback.

KS2: To create a short video to demonstrate how to give positive feedback to an alien who has just arrived in their class from Planet Venturas.

KS3: To be able to feed back to another young person on a project or task they have undertaken.

KS1

3. Create a puppet show to illustrate one puppet talking to another about a project they have given in. Make it silly but demonstrate all the things you DO NOT want the children to say.

4. Set the children a challenge – to spot all the mistakes or wrong ways you do things.

5. Read the story *Thanks for the Feedback* by Julia Cook.

6. Discuss how it can feel when people feed back good things about your work, and how it feels when they feed back things that you should think about or change.

7. Notice which feedback RJ's teacher gave him first; which feedback did she give him most of?

8. Once you have finished, ask the children how the puppet who had given in the project would feel. Discuss if making someone feel that way is useful. Pose the question: what is the point of feedback?

9. Share the hamburger analogy with the children. When you feed back, think of a hamburger: the top part of the bun, the beefburger in the middle and then the bottom part of the bun. The top part of the bun represents something you liked – that comes first; the beefburger is something that they need to improve, think about or alter to make it better; and the bottom part of the bun is something else you like. If you really really liked something they did then you can share that – this would be the sesame seeds on the top of the bun – really special!

10. Ask the children to use the puppets to show how to give feedback using the hamburger analogy.

11. Share what they thought of each other's puppet play – were there phrases they liked? If so, copy them down so people can use them again. Were there tones of voice they thought helpful? If so, share them and model them with the children.

12. Practise feedback in class. You could make a large beefburger poster and put words or phrases on it to help the children remember.

KS2

1. Share the video clip on constructive feedback with the children.

2. Discuss what they thought of the first picture compared to the last picture for a first grade child (Year 2).

3. Highlight that feedback is constructive – it shows or tells how to make something better and not just that it needs to be better.

4. Give the children the challenge – they have to produce a video to show how to give feedback to another person about their school work. This needs to be done for a new child who is coming into their class from the planet Venturas! They could use a drawing as in the video or a short story.

5.   Ask the children to work in small groups and work out their clip – ask the groups to share what they have done and for one of the other groups to give feedback.

6.   When the children are ready, ask them to film their clip and then share what they have all completed.

7.   When you watch the clips, can the children come up with the 5 Golden Rules of feedback?

     This might involve: always start with something you liked about the work, then move to say something about the effort or skill that person has used to produce the work, then ask a question – what do you think about . . . ? Is this what you wanted or can you think of a better way to do this? Then share something that they could extend or make more clear or more detailed . . .

KS3

1.   Share an episode of *The Great British Menu*, where the competitors are getting feedback from the Head Chef marking them.

2.   Discuss the pattern they are using and how this makes the contestants feel.

3.   Watch the video on constructive feedback and discuss the differences. For the chefs, there is no detailed discussion about how to improve things and for the constructive feedback there is greater use of sharing how to make something better. For the constructive feedback, the work is thought of as a series of drafts, for the cooking it is the end result.

4.   In pairs, ask the young people to come up with their top 10 tips for giving feedback to others.

5.   Share and discuss the strategies/rules they have come up with and then as a class ask the children to go and stand by the one they think is the most important. Take away the one that has the fewest people by it. Ask the children to vote again; once more, take away the strategy/rule that has the fewest people by it – continue to do this until only 3 are left. These are your top 3 strategies or rules.

6.   Ask the children to choose something that they would like feedback on from their partner.

7.   Share the feedback sheet and discuss – create your own if needed.

8.   Then ask the partners to work together to give feedback.

9.   Ask another pair to watch, and then feed back to the person giving the feedback on how they undertook the task. Or video this and then share it with the pair who had undertaken the feedback.

10. Share what they found and how this felt.

11. Why is being able to give feedback a good life skill?

RESOURCES

1. A range of hand puppets

2. Tablet computer

3. Feedback sheet

4. *Thanks for the Feedback* by Julia Cook

5. 'Critique and feedback – the story of Austin's butterfly', www.youtube.com/watch?v=hqh1MRWZjms

IMPORTANT POINTS

Being able to give positive feedback to another person is a useful skill in supporting others.

LEARNING LINKS

Friendships, collaboration, working together, teamwork, emotional literacy.

REFLECTION

Questions:

Positive comment from child:

Positive comment from adult:

LEARNING DIMENSIONS		SOCIAL & EMOTIONAL SKILLS	
Strategic awareness	🟧	Emotional literacy	
Learning relationships		Neuroscience	
Curiosity		Self-regulation	
Creativity	🟩	Self-development	🟩
Meaning making	🟧		
Changing & learning	🟩		
Resilience			

FEEDBACK SHEET

NAME		CLASS	DATE
NAME OF PERSON GIVING FEEDBACK		**WORK CHOSEN**	
Why did they choose to share this piece of work with you?			
What stood out in this piece of work?			
Why is this important?			
How did they do this well – what did you like and why?			
What did you think of the content of the work?			
What did you think of the layout of the work?			
What did you think of the illustrations?			
Which aspect of the work do they feel they could improve?			
Which part are they most pleased with?			

Specific words or phrases that would be good to weave into the conversation that demonstrate being positive:

The Beefburger Model

What did you like and why?

What could be changed, thought about or improved?

What did you like and why?

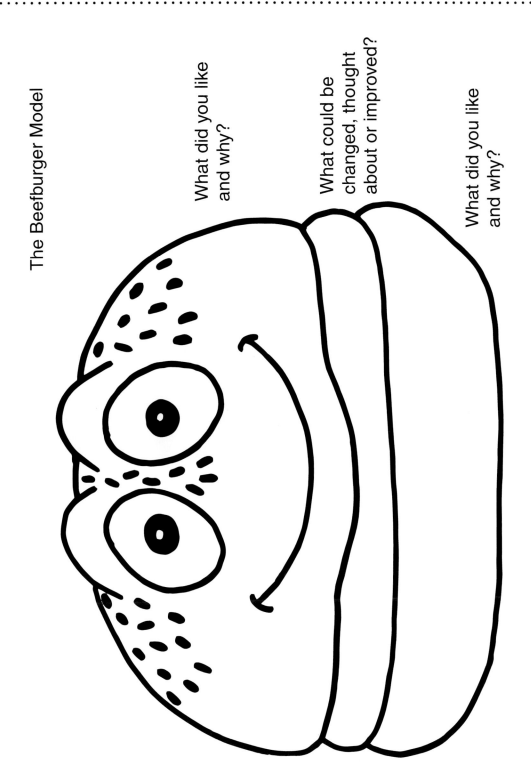

Sesame seeds - something special you would like to feed back.

Acknowledge when you have made a mistake

SESSION OBJECTIVES

To be able to share a mistake and understand how this has helped with your learning in some way.

To be able to acknowledge you have made a mistake and repair what has happened.

To be able to celebrate mistakes.

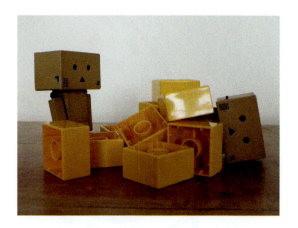

SESSION OUTCOMES

✓ To be able to understand that mistakes are important to learning.

✓ To be able to acknowledge a mistake and repair what happened.

✓ To understand that mistakes show that they are trying to grow and learn.

LESSON PLAN

➢ Ask the children to remember a time when they watched their baby make a mistake or get something wrong.

➢ How did this make the baby feel? How did their class parent respond? What did this response tell their class baby about making mistakes?

For those classrooms not able to undertake the Circles for Learning Project, video clips or photographs can be used to support the discussion around the topic and stimulate thoughts and ideas from the children and young people.

Task

KS1: To create a puppet show that shows how to repair a situation when you have made a mistake or got something wrong.

KS2/KS3: To be able to model how to acknowledge you have made a mistake and repair what has happened.

KS1

1. Act out doing something wrong – take the children to assembly when it is not on, get changed for P.E. when someone else is in the hall, etc.

2. Model how to show that you have made a mistake and apologise to the children.

3. Read the story *The Girl Who Never Made Mistakes* by Mark Pett.

4. Explore the idea of making mistakes with the children – share how you felt when you made the mistake.

5. Explore the different types of mistakes we can make – getting something wrong in our work, with friends, at home, when we are out, etc.

6. Discuss that when we make a mistake it is good to repair it if we can.

7. Discuss different ways to repair mistakes – saying sorry, doing something for someone, making a card, walking away and trying later, asking for help, practising, etc.

8. Ask the children to choose a card and then to create a puppet show to demonstrate how to repair the mistake.

9. Share the puppet shows and talk about what they show and how the people involved might feel.

KS2/KS3

1. Share the book *A Muddle of Mistakes* by J. K. Walton with the children.

2. Discuss the different types of mistake we can make – with friends, accidents, class work, when learning to do something new, etc.

3. Show the children the statement 'Saying sorry is being weak'. Ask the children to stand on the line with 'Saying sorry is being weak' at one end and 'Saying sorry shows strength' at the other. Ask children to explain their reasons.

4. Ask the children to work in pairs and come up with 3 different scenarios about making a mistake. Ask them to write each one on a separate piece of paper, e.g. 'You went to stay at your Dad's house and forgot to take you homework. Your Dad had to drive you back to your Mum's so you could get it.'

5. Lay all the mistakes out on the table and ask the children to walk round and then in their pairs choose one that they would like to work on to show how it could be repaired.

6. Give the children time to create a short act to show the mistake and how they could repair it.

7. Share the different scenarios the children have created and discuss what they have suggested. Focus on how people might feel and the different ways of repairing situations and how we can learn from mistakes both in and out of the classroom.

8. Remind the children of the constructive feedback video clip and the boy's butterfly.

RESOURCES

1. *A Muddle of Mistakes* by J. K. Walton

2. *The Girl Who Never Made Mistakes* by Mark Pett

3. Mistake cards

4. 'Critique and feedback – the story of Austin's butterfly', www.youtube.com/watch?v= hqh1MRWZjms

IMPORTANT POINTS

Making a mistake is an important part of learning. It shows you are brave enough to have a go. Mistakes can cause difficulties and it is important to be able to have the courage to mend or repair any damage your mistake may have made.

LEARNING LINKS

Friendships, collaboration, working together, social skills, emotional literacy, self-development.

REFLECTION

Questions:

Positive comment from child:

Positive comment from adult:

LEARNING DIMENSIONS		SOCIAL & EMOTIONAL SKILLS	
Strategic awareness		Emotional literacy	🟩
Learning relationships	🟩	Neuroscience	
Curiosity		Self-regulation	
Creativity		Self-development	🟩
Meaning making			
Changing & learning	🟩		
Resilience			

You visit your Grandparents' house and as you run into the garden you knock a vase over and it breaks.	You have borrowed your friend's hat and you realise you have lost it.
You forget to bring your friend's birthday card and present to school.	You forget to bring the project work you and your friend have been working on into school.
You drop your friend's toy in the playground and it breaks.	You get cross with your friend as you think that they have taken you toy, then you find it in your drawer.
You blame your friend for taking your reading book out of your bag, then your teacher gives you your book, which they had taken.	You go to get your P.E. kit and can't find it. You blame your Mum for taking it, then you find it on your peg at school.
Your friend won't play the game you want to play and you get cross and call them a rude name.	Your go to a friend's house for tea and knock your drink over; it goes all over the floor.
You are working on your art picture and you are really pleased with it, then you drop red paint in the middle of it.	You have written a great story on the computer but then you have to shut it down and you forget to save your work.
You are playing with your little sister on the beach; she has made a sandcastle and she is really happy with it. You trip over your spade and smash part of the castle.	You are helping your Dad wash the car; he gives you the hose pipe to hold as he washes the roof. You drop the hose and it squirts him with water.
You promised Mum you would tidy your room as Grandma is coming to stay and you forget.	You are playing in the playground when you spin round and knock over a child in reception.

Being kind and thoughtful

SESSION OBJECTIVES

To discuss how being kind and thoughtful feels to others and to ourselves.

To explore ways of celebrating acts of kindness.

SESSION OUTCOMES

✓ To understand how being kind and thoughtful makes others feel.

✓ To create ways to celebrate kindness within our community.

LESSON PLAN

➢ Ask the children how their class baby learns to be kind. Can they give examples of times when their class parent has modelled this behaviour, has praised this sort of behaviour or has supported kind and thoughtful behaviour?

For those classrooms not able to undertake the Circles for Learning Project, video clips or photographs can be used to support the discussion around the topic and stimulate thoughts and ideas from the children and young people.

Task

KS1: To create a way of celebrating kindness within the classroom.

KS2: To create an assembly to demonstrate the importance of kindness and how this can spread.

KS3: To create a kindness calendar month.

KS1

1. Read the story: *Have You Filled a Bucket Today?* to the children.

2. Talk about the things that people did to fill another person's bucket and how that made them feel.

3. Pose the question 'How can we celebrate kindness in our class?' Discuss the different ways that kindness could be celebrated.

- Giving a Warm Fuzzy to a child who has shown you kindness that day. This is a picture of a Warm Fuzzy creature that the children draw or write on the back of and give to the teacher – at the end of every day the teacher hands them out to children. This ensures that you can monitor what is happening.
- Kindness token -this is where, as a class, you design a kindness token that you make. When a child is kind to another, the child who is the receiver of the kindness collects a kindness token and writes what someone did for them. They then pass on the kindness by being kind to someone else.
- Kindness tree – this is where the class has a tree (large picture or a few real branches) and if someone has been kind to you, you write a luggage label to say thank you and give it to the teacher. At the end of the day the teacher gives out the labels and children can hang it on the tree.
- A note of kindness – this is where you ask children to draw a picture of someone else in the class – so that everyone has a partner and no one is forgotten. Once you have pictures of everyone, including the staff, you mount them in a big book and then if someone is kind or thoughtful you write a sticky note and stick them in the book to say thank you.

4. Work out which way you would like to celebrate and then set it up and help the children notice.

KS2

1. Read the book *Have You Filled a Bucket Today?* and discuss its message with the children.

2. Set up an Inquiry Line – One end of the line says 'Being kind to others makes you feel good' and the other end says 'Being kind to others has no impact on how you feel'.

3. Ask the children to stand on the line to show what they believe.

4. Ask each child to give an explanation/reason as to why they have chosen to stand in that place.

5. When everyone has spoken, give the children the chance to move and adjust their opinion.

6. Create a human bar chart with the children voting by standing next to the phrase that they believe in most.

7. Phrases to use:

- It is important to teach and celebrate kindness in school
- The job of schools is to teach academic subjects not kindness

- Kindness is something that should be taught at home by parents not teachers in school
- Being kind is not important

8. Hopefully the children have chosen that it is important to celebrate kindness in school. Explain to the children that you would like to create an assembly to share how important you all think it is and to encourage others to think about this.

9. Discuss the messages you would like the assembly to get across.

10. Create a list of ideas about how this could be done – discuss and then choose the one to undertake.

11. Have fun creating the assembly and then share with the school.

KS3

1. Share the pictures with the children. Ask them to work in groups to find out about the people and why they are special.

2. Ask each group to share with the class what they have found.

3. Explore what the overarching theme is.

4. Set up an Inquiry Line – One end of the line says 'Being kind to others makes you feel good.' And the other end says 'Being kind to others has no impact on how you feel.'

5. Ask the children to stand on the line to show what they believe.

6. Ask each child to give an explanation/reason as to why they have chosen to stand in that place.

7. When everyone has spoken give the children the chance to move and adjust their opinion.

8. Create a human bar chart with the children voting by standing next to the phrase that they believe in most.

9. Phrases to use:

- It is important to teach and celebrate kindness in school
- The job of schools is to teach academic subjects not kindness
- Kindness is something that should be taught at home by parents not teachers in school
- Being kind is not important

10. Ask the children to share their ideas and reasons for choosing the statement they have.

11. Discuss the different viewpoints.

12. Explain to the children that you want them to work in groups to create a calendar with a kindness that can be undertaken each day by the person reading it.

13. Share the calendars and choose one to have in the classroom. Ask the children to choose one of the days to perform that kindness and feed back to the class.

RESOURCES

1. Blank calendar month

2. Warm Fuzzies

3. Kindness tokens

4. Different sized buckets

5. *Have You Filled a Bucket Today?* by Carol McCloud

6. Pictures of famous people who made a difference in the world by their kindness:

   Oskar Schindler, Mother Teresa, Desmond Doss, Abraham Lincoln, Ivan Fernandez, the villagers of Eyam in Derbyshire, the Christians who encircled a group of Muslims in Tahrir Square in 2011, elderly Fukushima volunteers, the Good Samaritan

IMPORTANT POINTS

Being kind and thoughtful is catching.

LEARNING LINKS

Friendships, working together, sense of self, collaboration, emotional literacy.

REFLECTION

Questions:

Positive comment from child:

Positive comment from adult:

LEARNING DIMENSIONS		SOCIAL & EMOTIONAL SKILLS	
Strategic awareness		Emotional literacy	🟩
Learning relationships	🟩	Neuroscience	
Curiosity		Self-regulation	
Creativity	🟧	Self-development	🟩
Meaning making			
Changing & learning	🟧		
Resilience			

Warm Fuzzies

Kindness Tree Label

KINDNESS CURRENCY

Thank you for being so kind today. You've brightened my world in a very special way.

PASS IT ON

Pass this token to someone who is especially kind to you.

Calendar Month

Monday	Tuesday	Wednesday	Thursday	Friday	Saturday	Sunday

Being able to welcome the ideas of others

SESSION OBJECTIVES

To be able to demonstrate active listening and understand the importance of welcoming new ideas.

SESSION OUTCOMES

✓ To be able to explain why being open to new ideas is a useful skill to possess.

✓ To be able to model being open to someone's idea and demonstrate active listening.

LESSON PLAN

➢ Ask the children to remember a time when their class parent talked about the role of a parent and how they felt about this.

➢ Discuss how a parent knows how to be a parent, what they do when they don't know and how they work with their partner – who may have different ways of dealing with things.

For those classrooms not able to undertake the Circles for Learning Project, video clips or photographs can be used to support the discussion around the topic and stimulate thoughts and ideas from the children and young people.

Task

KS1: To work creatively together to come up with 100 things you can do with a toilet roll tube/ paper clip/elastic band/ice cream tub, etc.

KS2: To create an ideas jigsaw.

KS3: To create a radio advert to sell the 'generating new ideas' app.

KS1

1. Set the children a challenge to work together and come up with 100 ideas of things you could do with – a toilet roll, a paper clip, an elastic band or a yoghurt pot.

2. Think together and create a list and share with the children that one idea can often spark another. You need to allow them to be creative so all mad ideas count in this exercise!

3. Discuss what an idea is and come up with a variety of descriptions together.

4. Read the children *What Do You Do with an Idea?* by Kobi Yamada.

5. Ask them to draw a picture with their idea in a seed pod and then as a class write a recipe for the seed to grow and flourish.

    Carefully look after the seed – it is very precious
    Plant the seed in fertile soil where it can start to grow
    Water the seed with belief and love
    Feed the seed with energy and excitement
    Shelter the seed from negative comments
    Protect the seed from people who have no imagination
    Watch the seed with imagination and creativity
    Share the new idea with people and let them admire and smile

KS2

1. Ask the children to work in pairs and give them the blank jigsaw sheet.

2. Ask them to choose one of the following objects: paper clip, elastic band, piece of string, yoghurt pot, toilet roll or a plastic bottle top.

3. Ask them to think of 24 things that they can do with it, writing each idea on a blank jigsaw piece.

4. Once they have finished, place the jigsaws on the desk and then ask each pair to walk around and write on the paper next to the jigsaw their favourite idea from the jigsaw.

5. Share what they children have found – this could be that one idea leads to another, that working together stimulates ideas, that the wacky ideas lead to other ideas, that all ideas are useful but some are just better than others, etc.

6. Share with the children the book *What Do You Do with an Idea?* by Kobi Yamada.

7. Discuss and share ways that people can support ideas and ways that people can crush them. Come up with crushing words and lifting words that people can use.

KS3

1. Ask the children to work in groups and explain that their task is to create a radio advert for a new app that generates ideas.

2. Listen to a radio advert and highlight what the important points are that it gets across.

    *   Special phrase – e.g. 'have a break'
    *   Song or rhyme that you keep hearing after the advert
    *   Sounds that remind you of the product
    *   Uses the product name a lot
    *   Highlights why you need it

3. Share/decide together what the success criteria for the advert will be and create a tick list.

4. Ask the groups to work on the advert and then share how they are doing.

5. Support their demonstration by asking for constructive feedback from another group.

6. Record the adverts and share together.

7. Discuss how it feels when you have an idea – was it easy to share with the group, how did the group respond?

8. Create a list of crushing or listing words and phrases that can be used when an idea is shared.

RESOURCES

1. Large sheet of paper and pens

2. Jigsaw template

3. Tablet computer

4. *What Do You Do with an Idea?* by Kobi Yamada

IMPORTANT POINTS

Welcoming new ideas is a skill that can support collaboration and working with others.

Being open to new ideas can support teamwork and ensure that the team doesn't become stuck with a task.

LEARNING LINKS

Working together, collaboration, friendship, emotional literacy, teamwork, solution-focused problem solving.

REFLECTION

Questions:

Positive comment from child:

Positive comment from adult:

LEARNING DIMENSIONS		SOCIAL & EMOTIONAL SKILLS	
Strategic awareness	🟧	Emotional literacy	🟧
Learning relationships	🟩	Neuroscience	
Curiosity		Self-regulation	
Creativity	🟧	Self-development	🟩
Meaning making			
Changing & learning			
Resilience			

Chapter 4

Participation

TAKING PART AND HAVING
A GO   115

INCLUDING EVERYONE   120

WORKING TOGETHER   127

BUILDING YOUR CONFIDENCE   134

RESILIENCE   140

FOCUSING AND
CONCENTRATION   144

Taking part and having a go

SESSION OBJECTIVES

To explore the importance of taking part in an activity and having a go.

To explore some of the obstacles to joining in and having a go.

To understand how being brave and having courage can enable us to do things.

SESSION OUTCOMES

✓ To be able to share why some people might find taking part difficult and how this could be supported/made easier by others.

✓ To be able to talk about courage and share times when they have demonstrated this.

LESSON PLAN

➢ Ask the children to think of a time when they have watched their class baby being brave and having courage. Share what they noticed and what they feel enabled their class baby to behave in this way.

➢ How did their class parent support the baby?

For those classrooms not able to undertake the Circles for Learning Project, video clips or photographs can be used to support the discussion around the topic and stimulate thoughts and ideas from the children and young people.

Task

KS1/KS2: To create a picture that shows them doing something that took courage.

KS3: To create an individual gallery of pictures to show times of courage and being brave enough to have a go.

KS1/KS2

1. Introduce the word 'courage' and ask the children to share what they believe it means.

2. Ask them to work in pairs and share with their partner a time when they were courageous.

3. Ask the partners to feed back to the group about the time when their partner was courageous.

4. Share the book *Courage* by Bernard Waber.

5. Discuss the different types of courage that he shares and then add to these the different types of courage the children have shown.

6. Select aspects of courageousness that highlight joining in or having a go and ask the children to share an example of a time when they haven't wanted to join in but did or when they didn't want to have a go but did.

7. Ask the children to draw a picture of a time they didn't want to join in but did or didn't want to have a go but did.

8. Make a class scrap book of the pictures – 'Our Courageous Choices'.

9. Share the book and then explore with the children – what enabled them to do it – add these things to their page.

10. Share the book *You Can Do It Bert* by Ole Könnecke.

KS3

1. Introduce the word 'courage' and ask the children to share what they believe it means.

2. Ask them to work in pairs and share with their partner a time when they were courageous.

3. Ask the partners to feed back to the group about the time when their partner was courageous.

4. Read the book *Courage* by Bernard Waber and discuss the different types of courage that the group has shown.

5. Ask the children to share what enabled them to be courageous at the time. Was it the fear of not doing it or what someone would say? Was it positive self-talk in their head – 'You can do this'? Was it the thought of how pleased a special person would be when they heard that they had done something?

6. Ask the children to draw or write the things that they have been courageous enough to do inside each of the picture frames.

7. Lay these on the table and ask the children to walk around silently and read what people have put.

8. Finish by highlighting the courage that they have all had to achieve the things they have and that no one thing used more courage than another; each is personal to the person undertaking the challenge.

RESOURCES

1. *Courage* by Bernard Waber

2. *You Can Do It Bert* by Ole Könnecke

3. Picture frames

IMPORTANT POINTS

To have a go at something new takes courage.

Positive self-talk can support us when we need to be brave and have a go. Negative self-talk can stop us from taking part in something.

LEARNING LINKS

Self-development, self-esteem, social competencies, working with others, emotional literacy.

REFLECTION

Questions:

Positive comment from child:

Positive comment from adult:

LEARNING DIMENSIONS		SOCIAL & EMOTIONAL SKILLS	
Strategic awareness	🟧	Emotional literacy	
Learning relationships		Neuroscience	
Curiosity		Self-regulation	
Creativity	🟩	Self-development	🟩
Meaning making	🟧		
Changing & learning	🟩		
Resilience			

MY ASSETS

Including everyone

SESSION OBJECTIVES

To explore how our behaviour towards others can make people feel.

To understand that excluding people has an impact on their wellbeing.

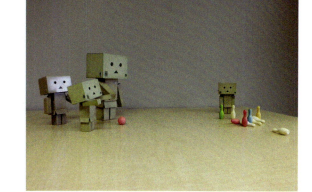

SESSION OUTCOMES

✓ To explore the impact our behaviour has on others and take responsibility for how we make others feel.

✓ To explore how being left out of a group can make people feel, and what they can do to challenge or help.

✓ To understand the terms inclusion and exclusion and be able to explain how they can make people feel and what they can do about it.

LESSON PLAN

➢ Ask the children to think about how they would like their class baby to be treated at school.

➢ As a parent how would they feel if their child was excluded from a group?

For those classrooms not able to undertake the Circles for Learning Project, video clips or photographs can be used to support the discussion around the topic and stimulate thoughts and ideas from the children and young people.

Task

KS1: To create a story using small world figures to show how to help if someone is left out of a game or activity.

KS2/KS3: To create a photograph and or piece of art work to show exclusion and inclusion and how this can make people feel.

KS1

1. Ask the children to work in pairs. Give each pair a picture and ask them to share with the group what they think the picture is about.

2. Choose one of the pictures and ask the children what the individual objects might be thinking – write their thoughts above them in thinking bubbles. Leave the 'lone' object until last.

3. Discuss the different ideas that come up. Find out what the children think.

4. Ask if any of the children can share a time when they were in the position of being in a group and knowing that someone was being left out or excluded. Let them share their thoughts – praise their courage for sharing something that is hard to think about. (Ask the children to share the story without naming people as it is not about naming and shaming – it is to illustrate a point or action.)

5. Ask for ideas about what to do when you are in that position – explore the consequences of those actions.

6. Share a time when you as an adult have not noticed or been able to do something – to show that we all make mistakes or do things that we regret.

7. Ask each child to find the best strategy for them to use if they experience being in a group that has excluded someone.

8. Share the story *Strictly No Elephants* by Lisa Mantchev and explore how the different people felt and what they did.

KS2/KS3

1. Ask the children to work in pairs. Give each pair a picture and ask them to share with the group what they think the picture is about.

2. Ask them to write the thoughts in thinking bubbles above the head of each object.

3. Share the ideas the children have come up with and explore.

4. Can any of the children share a time when this happened to them? Remind them to keep this general and not to mention names or individual people.

5. Explore how it felt from both the group's point of view and the excluded person's point of view.

6. Ask for strategies that might help anyone in the group who feels uncomfortable and wants to do something about the situation and also for the excluded person exploring things that they could do.

7. Remind the children about the Thoughts, Feelings, Actions Triangle and how this might help to understand the actions of people as well as support them if they want to change them.

8. Share with the children 'The Bystander Effect', www.youtube.com/watch?v= Wy6eUTLzcU4

9. Discuss this effect and what it means. How can this way of being be challenged? Now the children know this, is it an excuse not to do something or the answer to help them change?

10. Ask the children to create a photograph or piece of artwork to show what exclusion or being left out can be like either for someone in the group or the excluded person.

11. Set up a silent exhibition where the children can share their work. Leave clipboards with paper by each piece of artwork for the viewers to leave comments about the work and why they liked it.

RESOURCES

1. Photographs showing exclusion

2. Small world figures

3. Art materials

4. *Strictly No Elephants* by Lisa Mantchev

5. Thoughts, Feelings, Actions Triangle

6. 'The bystander effect', www.youtube.com/watch?v=Wy6eUTLzcU4

IMPORTANT POINTS

We make choices about how we behave and our behaviour affects other people and how they feel.

LEARNING LINKS

Social competencies, working together, emotional literacy, inclusion, responsibility.

REFLECTION

Questions:

Positive comment from child:

Positive comment from adult:

LEARNING DIMENSIONS		SOCIAL & EMOTIONAL SKILLS	
Strategic awareness	🟧	Emotional literacy	
Learning relationships		Neuroscience	
Curiosity		Self-regulation	
Creativity	🟩	Self-development	🟩
Meaning making	🟧		
Changing & learning	🟩		
Resilience			

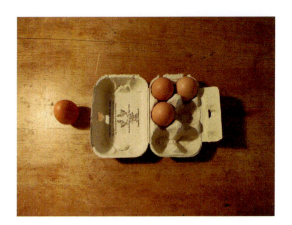

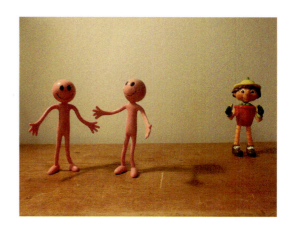

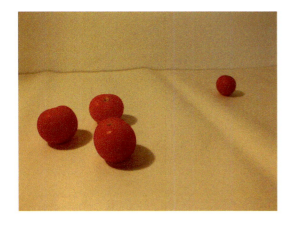

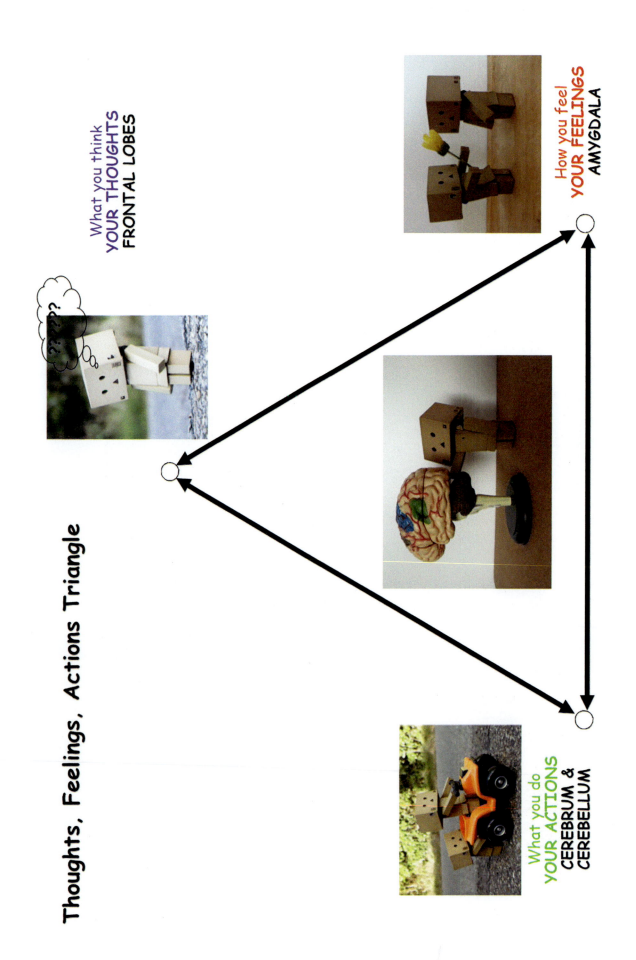

Thoughts, Feelings, Actions Triangle

What you think
YOUR THOUGHTS
FRONTAL LOBES

How you feel
YOUR FEELINGS
AMYGDALA

What you do
YOUR ACTIONS
CEREBRUM &
CEREBELLUM

Working together

SESSION OBJECTIVES

To explore the skills we need if we are to work with others successfully.

SESSION OUTCOMES

✓ To identify the skills needed to work with others.

✓ To be able to watch others interact and then feed back in a positive way the skills they used to make the work successful.

LESSON PLAN

1. Ask the children to describe a time when they watched their class parent and class baby work together to achieve something. What skills did they observe being used?

For those classrooms not able to undertake the Circles for Learning Project, video clips or photographs can be used to support the discussion around the topic and stimulate thoughts and ideas from the children and young people.

Task

KS1: To create an assembly that shows the importance of working together.

KS2: As a class to create a 'Skills for Working Together' card game.

KS3: To be able to give positive feedback to another young person on their skills in working with others.

KS1

1. Lay out a selection of pictures of animals working together and ask the children to walk around and have a look at them. Ask them to spot the theme that the pictures show.

2. Lay the pictures out on the floor at the front of the classroom and ask the children to stand by the picture that they like the most – creating a human bar chart.

3.   Show this on the board as a bar chart.

4.   Explain to the children that for the rest of the week you and they are going to be watching out for people working together. When you see this you are going to take a picture as a way of collecting the ways people can work together.

5.   Ask the children to think of all the different ways people work together in and around school – start a long list in the classroom for people to add to whenever they think of something.

6.   Point out different ways that you see in the classroom before you take a photo.

7.   Print off the photos and create a montage on one of the boards in the classroom.

8.   Share the book *Farmer Herman and the Flooding Barn* by Jason Weber with the children.

9.   At the end of the week, reflect on what you have found and ask the children to share their thoughts and experiences.

10. Have people worked together more this week? Why do they think this is? How can they keep this up? How can they spread the word about how good it is to support and work with each other? What skills have they used in working together?

11. Add the skills used to the montage.

12. Pick up on the idea to share this concept in assembly.

13. Ask the children to help create an assembly to show how helping each other has made them all feel.

14. Use the *Farmer Herman* book and act out the story to show in assembly to the other children in school. Explain to the children that the story is based on a true event.

15. Explain that you want everyone to take part in one way or another.

16. Create and have fun sharing.

KS2

1.   Lay out a selection of pictures of animals working together and ask the children to walk around and have a look at them. Ask them to spot the theme that the pictures show.

2.   Explain to the children that for the rest of the week you are going to be watching out for people working together and when you see this you are going to take a picture as a way of collecting the ways people can work together.

3.   Ask the children to think of all the different ways people work together in and around school – start a long list in the classroom for people to add to whenever they think of something.

4.   Point out different ways that you see in the classroom before you take a photo.

5.   Print off the photos and create a montage on one of the boards in the classroom.

6.   Share the book *Farmer Herman and the Flooding Barn* by Jason Weber with the children. Explain to the children that this is based on a true story.

7.   At the end of the week reflect on what you have found and ask the children to share their thoughts and experiences.

8.   Have people worked together more this week? Why do they think this is? How can they keep this up? How can they spread the word about how good it is to support and work with each other? What skills have they used in working together?

9.   Add the skills used to the montage.

10. Ask the children to work in small groups and set the challenge that you would like them to design and then make a card game that shows the skills needed for working together. Ask the children to think of as many card games as they can – Snap, Pairs, Happy Families, Top Trumps. Play the games and then discuss if they could be used to make the game look at skills for working together.

11. Try out the games and allow the children from one group to give constructive feedback to their partner group.

12. Enjoy playing.

KS3

1.   Ask the children to work in pairs and give them a photo showing people working together. Ask the pairs to come up with as many skills as they can that support working together in 60 seconds.

2.   Share the skills that the group has come up with and start a list.

3.   Explore how these skills are learnt, practised and become automatic.

4.   Explore what good constructive feedback might be and how the person receiving this might feel.

5.   Explore how a good coach might support someone learning a new skill. Do they concentrate on the right or wrong way to do something?

6.   Watch the video 'Austin's Butterfly', www.youtube.com/watch?v=hqh1MRWZjms

7. Explain to the children that they are going to practise using this model to support each other develop and strengthen the skills of working together.

8. Explain to the children that they are going to work in small groups on a task together and that they will be watched by another group which will be their support group.

9. Each person in the support group will watch one of the group and note down the skills they are using to work in the group.

10. As a class you will create a tally chart showing the skills that you think are the most important when working in a group.

11. The observer will mark each skill you use so that at the end of the observation they will be able to feed back to their person the skills they have used, thus showing their strengths, and also support them in developing or strengthening other skills that they have used less often.

12. Work with the children to create a top 10 list of skills needed to work successfully in a group. Photocopy so that each person has a sheet to mark for the person they are observing.

13. Ask the children to get into groups of 4 children and then pair up the groups, naming them A or B.

14. Ask each group to agree who they will be observing during the group task.

15. Ask group A to undertake the group task first and group B to observe.

16. When the task is complete, ask each person to feed back to the person they observed, focusing on what they did well and then which areas they could strengthen and how.

17. Ask group B to undertake the group task with group A observing.

18. Group A to feed back to each person as previously.

19. Come back as a group and share what they have learnt.

RESOURCES

1. Tablet computer

2. Card

3. Glue

4. *Farmer Herman and the Flooding Barn* by Jason Weber

5. A collection of pictures showing animals working together

6. Card games – Snap, Pairs, Happy Families, Top Trumps

7. Skills sheet

8. 'Critique and feedback – the story of Austin's butterfly', www.youtube.com/watch?v=hqh1MRWZjms

IMPORTANT POINTS

Being able to work with others uses a variety of skills and attitudes.

Being able to work with others well impacts on learning and life.

LEARNING LINKS

Social competencies, teamwork, emotional literacy, friendships, learning, group work.

REFLECTION

Questions:

Positive comment from child:

Positive comment from adult:

LEARNING DIMENSIONS		SOCIAL & EMOTIONAL SKILLS	
Strategic awareness	🟧	Emotional literacy	
Learning relationships		Neuroscience	
Curiosity		Self-regulation	
Creativity	🟩	Self-development	🟩
Meaning making	🟧		
Changing & learning	🟩		
Resilience			

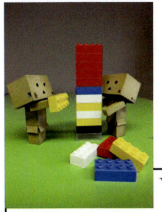

WORKING TOGETHER

SKILLS	TALLY	TOTAL

Building your confidence

SESSION OBJECTIVES

To understand that confidence is a belief that can grow and decline depending upon our own thinking and how we perceive things.

SESSION OUTCOMES

✓ To understand our confidence can grow and decline and that it can be high in one area and low in another.

LESSON PLAN

➢ Ask the children to describe a time when their class baby learnt how to do something new. Ask them to share the process their baby went through to be able to learn the new activity.

➢ How did their confidence alter as they were learning?

For those classrooms not able to undertake the Circles for Learning Project, video clips or photographs can be used to support the discussion around the topic and stimulate thoughts and ideas from the children and young people.

Task

KS1/KS2: To create a 'confidence catcher'.
KS3: To create a confidence board sharing the 10 items about confidence requested.

KS1/KS2

1. Introduce the word CONFIDENCE and ask the children to describe what it means.

2. Can they share something they are confident in? How did they become confident in this? Who helped them? How did they help them?

3. Pose the question: How does confidence grow?

4. Can they share something they are not confident in YET?

5. Show the children a dream catcher and explain that they are going to make a confidence catcher. The confidence catcher will catch and hold all the things that they have the confidence to do so that, when they wobble, they can look at it and know that it's just that they can't do something YET but if they keep going they will soon learn.

6. Lay out the art materials, ribbons, wool, string, and sparkly thread, and other collage things for the children to use.

7. Ask the children to draw around the cardboard template and then cut out the outer circles and the circle in the middle.

8. Mark the dots on both.

9. Put the card on some blue tack and then push a pencil through the card where the holes are. There should be 16 holes around the outside of the inner circle. There are 16 holes around the inside of the outer ring and then one hole at the top to hang the confidence catcher and 5 at the bottom to hang things from.

10. On the inner circle write a message to help when your confidence starts to wobble.

11. Join the inner circle to the outer ring by joining the holes with wool (see figure).

12. Decorate with beads, feathers, ribbons, bows and other craft items.

13. Hang in the classroom and as children achieve things fill in a luggage label and tie it to the confidence catcher.

KS3

1. Ask the children to work in pairs and :

   - Define the word CONFIDENCE
   - Research a picture that they think captures the meaning of the word
   - Research a quote that they feel would support them if their confidence wobbled
   - Find a photograph of someone being confident or doing something confidently
   - Find a quote from a famous person about confidence
   - Find a song or piece of music that makes them feel confident
   - Create or find a poem about confidence – either their own creation or one that inspires them
   - Share a photograph of themselves doing something that they feel confident about
   - Create a short story sharing a time when their confidence grew and they were able to do something new.
   - Create an acrostic poem about confidence

2.   When they have gathered their 10 confidence items, ask them to display them for others to see.

3.   Set up the exhibitions as an art gallery and ask the children to walk around and observe in silence.

4.   Return to the group and ask the children to share their thoughts and ideas.

5.   What 3 things will they take away from the lesson?

RESOURCES

1.   Luggage tags

2.   Willow sticks or hoops or card circles

3.   Ribbons, sparkly thread, string, beads, stars, feathers and other craft items

4.   Large paper (A5)

5.   Pens, pencils or paints

6.   Confidence catcher

IMPORTANT POINTS

The way we think impacts on what we can do. If we think we can't, we won't; if we think we can, we will.

LEARNING LINKS

Emotional literacy, sense of self, self-esteem, achievements, positive thinking.

REFLECTION

Questions:

Positive comment from child:

Positive comment from adult:

LEARNING DIMENSIONS		SOCIAL & EMOTIONAL SKILLS	
Strategic awareness	🟧	Emotional literacy	
Learning relationships		Neuroscience	
Curiosity		Self-regulation	
Creativity	🟩	Self-development	🟩
Meaning making	🟧		
Changing & learning	🟩		
Resilience			

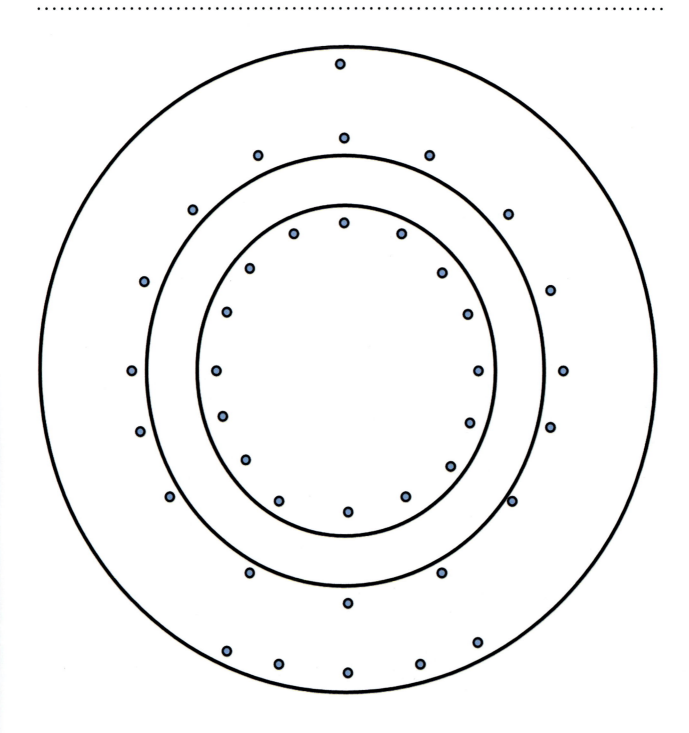

Confidence Catcher

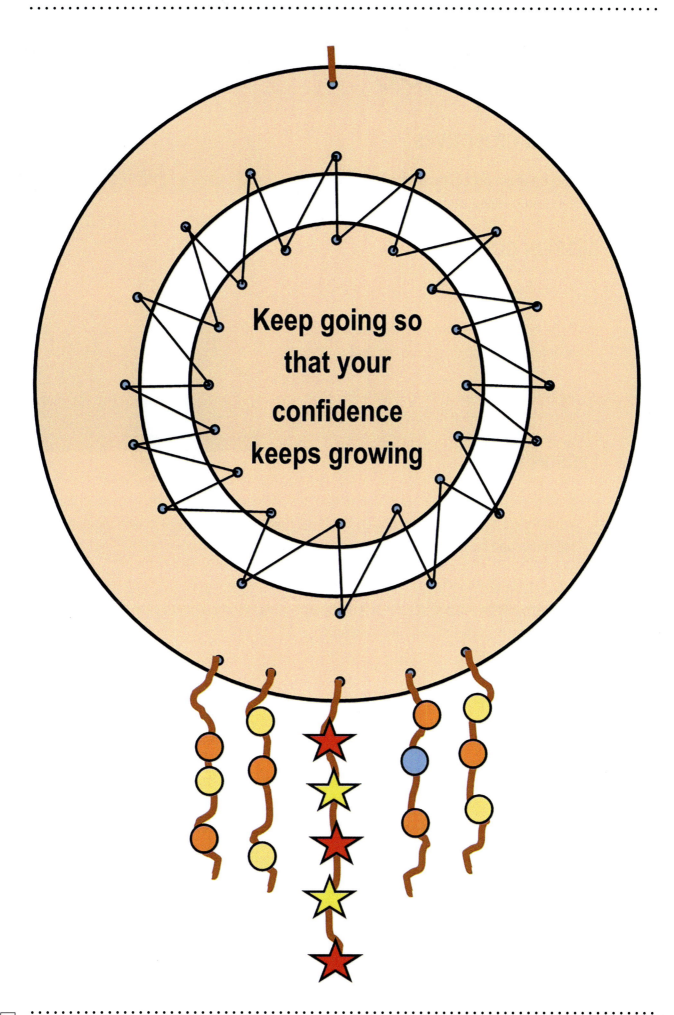

Keep going so that your confidence keeps growing

Resilience

SESSION OBJECTIVES

To explore the concept of resilience and identify helpful and unhelpful strategies to build resilience.

SESSION OUTCOMES

✓ To be able to share a definition of resilience.

✓ To be able to share strategies that we use that support us in becoming more resilient.

✓ To be able to identify new strategies that we would like to develop to support our resilience.

LESSON PLAN

➢ Ask the children to remember a time when their class baby was learning to crawl or walk. What things made them keep going? What did their class parent do if everything became too much and they became flooded by a strong emotion?

For those classrooms not able to undertake the Circles for Learning Project, video clips or photographs can be used to support the discussion around the topic and stimulate thoughts and ideas from the children and young people.

Task

KS1: To identify helpful and unhelpful thinking in times of stress.

KS2: To create an exhibition on resilience.

KS3: To create an information phrase that shows what resilience is and strategies to support us in times of stress.

KS1

1. Ask the children what they think the word 'resilience' means. Can they give examples of someone being resilient?

2. Share the story *The Hugging Tree* by Jill Neimark.

3. What sort of things allow the tree to keep growing and holding on?

4. Show the children a Weeble – a toy which wobbles but won't fall over; it keeps bouncing back. Explain that this is like resilience – you bounce back. The question is what enables you to bounce back up.

5. Ask the children to work in pairs and come up with a sentence that says what resilience is and 1 strategy that can help you be resilient or bounce back.

6. Share the ideas and create a class definition and a list of helpful strategies that you can use. Next to this, make a list of unhelpful strategies.

    Helpful: Positive self-talk, reminding yourself of what you have achieved, asking for help if you need it, problem solving, flexible thinking, learning from mistakes, allowing yourself to make mistakes, being positive, believing that you can do it etc.

    Unhelpful: Negative self-talk, not asking for help, getting cross when you make a mistake, thinking that you can't do something, not believing in yourself, forgetting all the things you have managed etc.

7. Ask the children to share which strategy they think they are best at and then one that they would like help to work on.

8. Write their challenge on a sticky note and put it on their desks to remind them which strategy they are growing.

9. Check in with children to see how they are doing with their challenge.

KS2

1. Ask the children to work in pairs and complete the challenge and create a display/ exhibition of their collection:

    *   A definition of 'resilience'
    *   A picture/photograph showing resilience
    *   A story/book that tells about resilience
    *   A poem on resilience
    *   A quote that helps you be resilient
    *   A list of 6 skills that resilient people have.
    *   An acrostic poem about resilience that they have made
    *   A picture they have created of themselves being resilient
    *   A recipe for growing resilience that they have created
    *   A cartoon drawing of the 'Rubber Band Kids', a group of kids who are resilient and their arch enemy the Resilience Eater

2. When the children have collected all their objects ask them to set up a display/exhibition.

3. Ask the children to view the exhibition in silence.

4. Join back together and share what they have learnt. What they enjoyed? what they are going to think about?

KS3

1. Ask the children to work in pairs and research resilience.

2. Ask them to bring to the group:

    •   A definition they like
    •   A photograph they feel shows the word in action
    •   6 skills resilient people have

3. Discuss what they have found and what they have learnt.

4. Ask the children to work in pairs and to choose a short phrase and turn this into an acrostic list of how to be resilient.

    R – Remember to be flexible with your thinking
    E – Embrace mistakes they help us learn
    S – Sometimes we need to ask for help knowing when is strong not weak
    I – If you can find something positive or funny in a bad situation then go for it.
    L – Life is normally good but everyone has difficult times – that is normal
    I – Identify your strengths – you have lots and some of these will help you
    E – Ensure you always challenge the negative self-talk – keep it positive
    N – Never let yourself get out of control – keep calm
    T – Try and think about the problem in lots of ways – one of them will work

5. Ask the children to use a word or phrase they have come up with from their research. It could be 'bounce back', rubber band thinking, etc.

6. Share the work when they have completed it.

7. Finish by asking the children for something they have learnt, something that they are going to think about and a strategy they want to develop.

RESOURCES

1. 'Resilience in kids', www.youtube.com/watch?v=HYsRGeOtfZc

2. *The Hugging Tree* by Jill Neimark

3. Access to the internet

IMPORTANT POINTS

Being resilient involves a group of skills that can all be learnt, practised and strengthened.

LEARNING LINKS

Self-development, emotional literacy, working together, social competencies, achievement and learning.

REFLECTION

Questions:

Positive comment from child:

Positive comment from adult:

LEARNING DIMENSIONS		SOCIAL & EMOTIONAL SKILLS	
Strategic awareness	🟧	Emotional literacy	
Learning relationships		Neuroscience	
Curiosity		Self-regulation	
Creativity	🟩	Self-development	🟩
Meaning making	🟧		
Changing & learning	🟩		
Resilience			

Focusing and concentration

SESSION OBJECTIVES

To explore how to support concentration and focus.

SESSION OUTCOMES

✓ To enable children and young people to discuss what focus and concentration mean to them.

✓ To enable children and young people to share a range of strategies that enable them to focus and concentrate.

LESSON PLAN

➢ Ask the children to share a time when they watched their class baby focus and concentrate on a task. What was their motivation? What enabled them to focus and concentrate? How did their class parent support them?

For those classrooms not able to undertake the Circles for Learning Project, video clips or photographs can be used to support the discussion around the topic and stimulate thoughts and ideas from the children and young people.

Task

KS1: To be able to share a time when they feel they have concentrated on something and to describe what that felt like.
To create a 'Puppy Brain' cartoon and 3 top tips for training.

KS2: To be able to describe the strategies they use to enter the 'Learning Zone' and to enable themselves to stay there and focus on a task.
To create a 'Steps to get into the Learning Zone' booklet.

KS3: To explore the concept of 'flow' and 'being in the zone'.
To create poster showing strategies for stay in the Learning Zone.

KS1

1. Act out a short sketch for the children showing you concentrating on a task and then being really distracted.

2. Ask the children what they saw and what they felt was going on.

3. Explore the concept of concentration and focus.

4. Ask the children to draw a picture of themselves when they are concentrating and to put words around the picture about what they need to do this. This could be being quiet, being interested, working with a friend etc.

5. Share the video of a puppy and point out how difficult it is for him to concentrate as he keeps getting distracted by other things.

6. Explain that the human brain is the same – it likes new things, and is very curious and so is easily distracted.

7. Ask the children to draw a 'Puppy Brain' cartoon, think of a name for their puppy brain and show it trying to concentrate and ignore distractions. What would be their 3 top tips for training their puppy brain?

8. Share the tips that they come up with.

9. Refer to these tips for puppy training when working in the classroom, explaining that, as with a puppy, the training has to happen often if they are to be able to learn the skill.

KS2

1. Share the two pictures with the children: Picture 1 – running around having fun in the playground. Picture 2 – quietly working in class.

2. Share the learning zone and put the pictures in the correct place.

3. Ask the children to work in pairs to share the strategies that they use to get themselves into the Learning Zone.

4. Write the strategies on the board to show the different ones used.

5. Ask the children to share what helps them to move from an excited place – playtime – to a quiet and thinking space – classroom time.

6. Ask one of the children to act like a curious puppy and give them the extendable lead to hold – let them run off and explore and then pull them back.

7. Pose the question – what do they do to bring their concentration back? A bit like the distracted puppy being pulled back.

8. Share with the children some different ways of doing this and explain that you are going to experiment over the next few days.

9. Explain to the children that you would like them to work in their pairs and create a 'Steps to get into the Learning Zone' booklet together.

10. This needs to show

    • The top 5 strategies that can be used
    • How to learn the strategies
    • Fun ways to practise the strategies
    • Sticker page to reward your efforts
    • A fun saying to help you learn the strategies
    • A before and after story showing why the strategies are useful
    • A cartoon character – Super Concentration and their enemy The Focus Eater
    • When the booklets are complete, lay them out on the desks with sticky notes and ask the children to go around and write one thing that they enjoyed about each booklet and one thing that the writers could focus on next time to improve their resource.

11. During the next few days, introduce a range of different ways to help children calm and focus after playtime. Try a singing bowl, visualisation, relaxation, breathing exercises, yoga poses, silent reading, reading a story etc.

12. Discuss which ones they found helpful and why.

KS3

1. Introduce the concept 'In the Zone' Explore when the children have felt themselves enter this zone. Name an activity that enables them to find 'flow'.

2. If possible ask the children to bring something to the next lesson that allows them to find this zone. Share the different activities that they would like to bring – they must be suitable for the classroom.

3. After the session, explore how they prepared themselves for their chosen activity.

4. What did they need to do to keep themselves in the zone?

5. Ask the children to create a poster/fold-out leaflet to show the step by step approach of how to get themselves into the zone and feel flow and to keep themselves there. At the end describe what it is like to be in the zone or to have experienced flow. This can be in words or in an art form.

6. Share and discuss what the children have created.

7. How did they learn this skill? How would they teach this skill to someone?

RESOURCES

1. Puppy walking video, www.youtube.com/watch?v=e651783C6_o

2. 'Flow' definition poster

3. Paper

4. Felt tips, pens and pencil, crayons

5. Extendable dog lead

6. Visualisation script

7. Relaxation script

8. Breathing exercises

9. Singing bowl

IMPORTANT POINTS

Being able to get yourself into the Learning Zone when you want or need is an important skill.

Maintaining focus and concentration is important and can be achieved with a range of techniques.

LEARNING LINKS

Concentration, effective learning skills, focus, enjoyment, self-regulation.

REFLECTION

Questions:

Positive comment from child:

Participation

Positive comment from adult:

LEARNING DIMENSIONS		SOCIAL & EMOTIONAL SKILLS	
Strategic awareness	🟧	Emotional literacy	
Learning relationships		Neuroscience	
Curiosity		Self-regulation	
Creativity	🟩	Self-development	🟩
Meaning making	🟧		
Changing & learning	🟩		
Resilience			

'Flow' is a term created by Mihály Csíkszentmihályi in 1975. It is a term used in positive psychology, and is also known as being 'in the zone'. It describes a mental state in which a person performing an activity is fully immersed in what they are doing and are fully involved, and enjoying the process of the activity. Flow is the complete absorption in what one does, and results in a loss of one's sense of space and time.

The Learning Zone

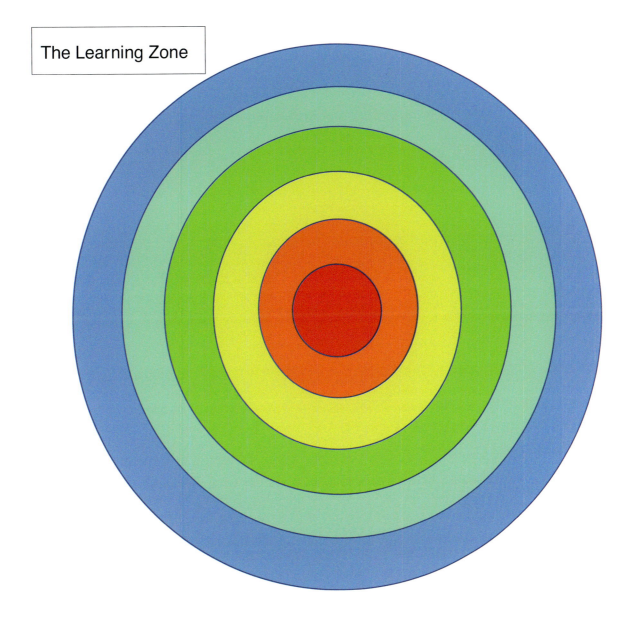

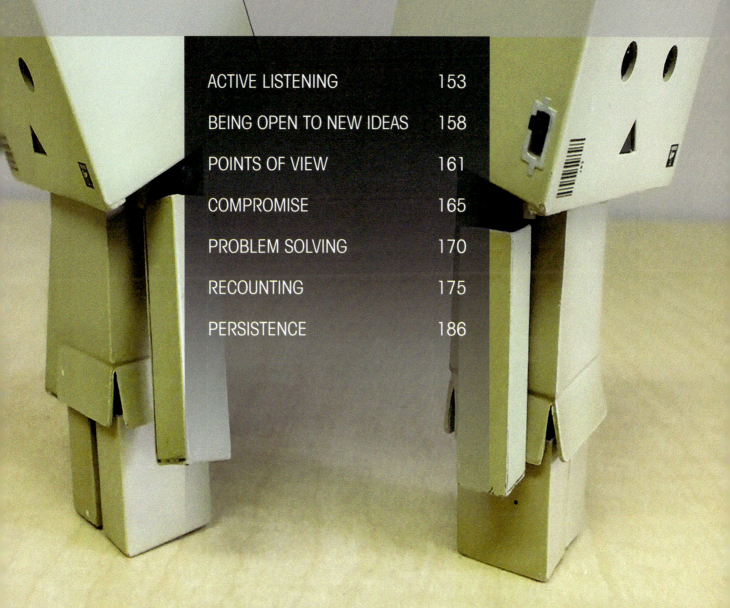

Chapter 5

Resolving conflict

ACTIVE LISTENING 153

BEING OPEN TO NEW IDEAS 158

POINTS OF VIEW 161

COMPROMISE 165

PROBLEM SOLVING 170

RECOUNTING 175

PERSISTENCE 186

Active listening

SESSION OBJECTIVES

To be able to demonstrate the skills of active listening.

SESSION OUTCOMES

✓ To be able to identify passive listening behaviours and active listening behaviours.

✓ To be able to demonstrate active listening behaviours when working with another.

LESSON PLAN

➢ Ask the children how their class baby may feel if they try to show something to their parent and they are preoccupied and don't take any notice. What happens if this is something that keeps happening rather than a single occurrence?

For those classrooms not able to undertake the Circles for Learning Project, video clips or photographs can be used to support the discussion around the topic and stimulate thoughts and ideas from the children and young people.

Task

KS1: To be able to identify behaviours of active listening and passive listening.
KS2: To interview another young person demonstrating active listening behaviours.
KS3: To create a short sketch to show the dangers of passive listening!

KS1

1.   Explain to the children that they are going to need to be detectives and observe a short play and then identify the things people are doing that make them good listeners.

2.   Divide the class into small groups and give them sticky notes to write on.

3.   Act out active listening with another adult in front of the children. Pause every once in a while so that they can write things down.

4.   If you can video the people involved in the acting, it enables you to use this later and highlight different skills or techniques used.

5. Help the children to identify good active listening skills and make a list of those that they have observed and identified: looking at the person speaking, open body language with your body pointing at the speaker, nodding or facial gestures, repeating back certain points to show you have heard and understood, asking questions, etc.

6. Ask the groups to work in pairs and try out some of these skills. While one pair is talking and listening, the other pair is noting down the skills they are using.

7. Highlight the skills being used in class over the next week or so and remind the children what to do. Support the children in observing and feeding back when other children are being active listeners. Make sure it stays positive and do not let the focus change to children who are not being active listeners.

KS2

1. Create a short video with either an adult or a few children showing active listening and passive listening mixed together.

2. Share the video with the children and ask them to work in pairs to write down active listening and passive listening behaviours on sticky notes as they watch. Put one behaviour on each sticky note.

3. Create a table on the board labelled 'Active Listening Behaviours' and 'Passive Listening Behaviours'.

4. Ask the children to place the sticky labels they have written on in the correct column.

5. Discuss what you have found – rewind the video so that the children can see the behaviours again. Add any that were not seen the first time.

6. Discuss how the person speaking feels when the listener is actively listening and when they are passively listening.

7. Ask the children to work in pairs and try out the different behaviours. Ask the first pair to share something that they have learnt to do which they are really proud of – the listener uses as many of the active listening behaviours as they can.

8. Share how the listener felt when being listened to in this way.

9. Now ask the children to share something they did on holiday which they enjoyed – ask the listeners to listen in a passive way.

10. Share how the listener felt when being listened to in this way.

11. Now ask the children to swap over so that the other pair has a chance to experience both ways of being listened to.

KS3

1. Ask the children to work in pairs and research passive listening behaviour and active listening behaviour.

2. Ask each pair to perform a short sketch showing listening to someone in a passive way and then, when you call out 'change', turn this into active listening.

3. Ask the audience to watch for active listening behaviours and passive listening behaviours and to record them.

4. Share the different behaviours they have identified.

5. Ask them to create a short sketch entitled 'The Dangers of Passive Listening!'

6. Put on a short performance showing the different sketches.

RESOURCES

1. 'Passive Listening Behaviours'

2. 'Active Listening Behaviours'

3. Video camera

IMPORTANT POINTS

Active listening is compiled of a range of behaviours and enables a much more in-depth conversation with another person.

LEARNING LINKS

Working with others, teamwork, friendships, relationships, self-development.

REFLECTION

Questions:

Positive comment from child:

Positive comment from adult:

LEARNING DIMENSIONS		SOCIAL & EMOTIONAL SKILLS	
Strategic awareness		Emotional literacy	🟩
Learning relationships	🟩	Neuroscience	
Curiosity		Self-regulation	
Creativity		Self-development	🟩
Meaning making			
Changing & learning	🟧		
Resilience	🟩		

Active Listening Behaviours	Passive Listening Behaviours
Paraphrasing to show understanding	Looking away from the person talking
Nonverbal cues which show understanding such as nodding, eye contact, and leaning forward	Nonverbal cues that show disinterest such as leaning back, arms folded, body turned away from speaker
Brief verbal affirmations like 'I see', 'I know', 'Sure', 'Thank you' or 'I understand'	Fiddling with hands or other objects
Summarising what the person has said to show you have heard them and understood	Not showing understanding of the speaker – just listening and saying nothing
Showing understanding of what the speaker is saying	No involvement with what the speaker is saying
Avoiding distracting gestures or fiddling with objects	Passive facial expressions that convey a lack of engagement
Not interrupting the speaker	Checking phone
Asking questions to show interest	
Facial expressions that show interest	

Being open to new ideas

SESSION OBJECTIVES

To be able to acknowledge and accept new ideas when working with others.

SESSION OUTCOMES

✓ To understand the importance of idea generation when working on projects or problem solving.

✓ To understand different points of view.

LESSON PLAN

➢ Ask the children to think about being a parent. What would it be like to have different ideas about ways of doing things from the child's other parent?

➢ How might the baby feel if parents kept arguing about how to do things and who was right?

For those classrooms not able to undertake the Circles for Learning Project, video clips or photographs can be used to support the discussion around the topic and stimulate thoughts and ideas from the children and young people.

Task

KS1: To draw an idea welcoming other ideas into the classroom.

KS2/KS3: To be able to generate a range of ideas as a team and then problem solve which one to use.

KS1

1. Ask the children to draw an idea.

2. Discuss what they think an idea looks like, what it needs to grow or what makes it shrivel up and lose its power.

3. How does the idea feel about other ideas coming to play? Ask them to think about a time when they had to share ideas and the children they were with liked the other person's idea more than theirs.

4. Share a problem with the children (this could be linked to a problem you have in the classroom) and ask them to write their idea on their idea picture and then to share with others.

5. Create an idea party with the other ideas children have generated.

6. Explore the different ideas and look at how they could all work. Choose the best idea for the problem. Discuss how lots of ideas give you more to choose from and are likely to mean you can find the best idea for the job. You can't have a party with just one idea!

KS2/KS3

1. Ask the children to work in small groups.

2. Set the groups a problem or a conundrum: make a plastic cup tower using a rubber band and 4 bits of string (you are not allowed to touch the cups with your hands) OR another teamwork problem-solving game.

3. Set each group off on their challenge – ask them to generate as many ideas for solving the problem as they can and list them on the problem page.

4. Choose their top 3 ideas and present them to the rest of the group, sharing why they chose them.

5. Ask the group to vote for the best idea for each group.

6. Ask the groups to go and make the solution and then share with the group.

7. Discuss as a group how ideas were accepted. How did this make people feel about sharing ideas?

8. How could ideas be accepted and then thought about? Think about the use of language, e.g., that's a good idea thank you, that's stupid, OK, how would you see that solving the problem, can you explain a bit more, that won't work etc.

9. List helpful language and unhelpful language.

RESOURCES

1. Resources for problems: 10 plastic cups per team, 2 elastic bands (large) , string, scissors, 4 pencils, 2 meter rulers

2. 'Cup stacking – team building exercise', www.youtube.com/watch?v=S-MTuGSTJR8

IMPORTANT POINTS

Being able to accept ideas and think about/analyse them is an important skill when working with others.

LEARNING LINKS

Working with others, friendships, teamwork, emotional literacy, self-development, problem solving.

REFLECTION

Questions:

Positive comment from child:

Positive comment from adult:

LEARNING DIMENSIONS		SOCIAL & EMOTIONAL SKILLS	
Strategic awareness		Emotional literacy	🟩
Learning relationships	🟩	Neuroscience	
Curiosity		Self-regulation	🟧
Creativity	🟩	Self-development	🟩
Meaning making			
Changing & learning	🟧		
Resilience	🟩		

Points of view

SESSION OBJECTIVES

To understand that different people can see and experience things in different ways.

SESSION OUTCOMES

✓ To be able to share how different people may feel about or understand an event.

LESSON PLAN

➤ Ask the children to think about when their class baby did something their parent didn't want them to do. What was their class baby thinking, what was the reason for what they were doing? What was their parent thinking? What was their reason for behaving as they did?

For those classrooms not able to undertake the Circles for Learning Project, video clips or photographs can be used to support the discussion around the topic and stimulate thoughts and ideas from the children and young people.

Task

KS1: In groups, make the masks and then act out a short well-known story and be able to talk about how their character felt.

KS2: As a group, create an interview showing how the different characters within a story felt.

KS3: To create a short sketch to show a social dilemma and how the different people felt.

KS1

1. Divide the class into small groups.

2. Read them a story.

3. Make masks for the characters and then ask them to act it out.

4. When acting, stop every once in a while and ask how a character might be feeling and why. If you used Goldilocks, then you might wonder how she felt when she entered the house of the bears or when she broke Baby bear's chair.

5. Help the children to see that the different characters feel different things. Baby bear would have been sad that his chair was broken, Daddy bear might have been angry that someone broke into his house, etc.

6. Ask the children to choose a character and then draw their picture and write a sentence underneath to show how they felt in the story.

KS2

1. Share a well-known story with the children. 'Hansel and Gretel' works well.

2. Ask the children to get into small groups and give each person a character from the story: Father, Stepmother, Witch, Hansel, Gretel. One person needs to be the interviewer.

3. It is useful to make masks for this as it helps the children get into character.

4. Ask the children to work as a team to come up with questions that the interviewer might ask the characters.

   Gretel – How did you feel when you went into the woods?
   Hansel – How did you feel when you knew your Father had gone home and left you in the woods.
   Father – How did you feel when your new wife suggested that you leave the children in the woods as you didn't have enough food to feed them?
   Stepmother – How did it feel to have so little money that you couldn't feed your family?

5. Ask each group to share their interviews.

6. Discuss the different people's points of view and how differently they saw the situation.

7. Share the book *The Tale of Two Beasts* by Fiona Roberton. When you have finished reading it to the children, pose the question – Who was lying? Discuss if anyone was actually lying or if they were just telling the story from their point of view.

8. Ask the children to write the story you have chosen from their character's point of view.

KS3

1. Share the social dilemma with the children and introduce the characters.

2. Divide the class into groups and ask each person in the group to take on a character.

3. Ask the groups to create a sketch that shows how the different characters are feeling and what they are thinking. This could be focused on meetings between different people or an interview with the papers or TV.

4. Share the different sketches and discuss what the children have found/noticed/ questioned.

5. What knowledge, thoughts or ideas will they take away from this exercise?

RESOURCES

1. *The Tale of Two Beasts* by Fiona Roberton

2. Story masks for your chosen book

3. Social dilemmas

IMPORTANT POINTS

Being able to think and understand how someone else experiences a situation is a vital skill in working with others.

LEARNING LINKS

Self-awareness, teamwork, friendships, emotional literacy, sense of self, empathy.

REFLECTION

Questions:

Positive comment from child:

Positive comment from adult:

LEARNING DIMENSIONS		SOCIAL & EMOTIONAL SKILLS	
Strategic awareness		Emotional literacy	🟩
Learning relationships	🟩	Neuroscience	
Curiosity		Self-regulation	🟧
Creativity	🟧	Self-development	🟩
Meaning making			
Changing & learning	🟧		
Resilience	🟩		

SOCIAL DILEMMAS	
The local school keeps getting broken into and vandalised.	**A group of young people keep shoplifting in the local corner shop**.

The local school keeps getting broken into and vandalised.

Caretaker – Mr Smith is very fed up as he is having to clear everything up and he isn't able to get on with the jobs he needs to.

Older lady who lives opposite the school. Mrs Silver is in her 80s and lives alone now her husband has died. She is frightened by the noises she hears at night and from the stories she reads about in the local paper.

Teenagers – Colin, Tam, Pete and Nim all live near the school and like to meet up outside the corner shop and have a laugh. People keep treating them as if it is them that keep vandalising the school.

Ted and Chaz are two teenagers who have been excluded from the school as the school is not able to meet their needs and they have been violent towards other children and staff. They are angry with the school and have been breaking in to wind people up.

Mr and Mrs Stevens own the corner shop and get on well with the teenagers as their son often hangs out with them.

Mrs Frant is the Head Teacher of the school. She is cross that the school keeps getting broken into and vandalised. She and her staff have worked hard to create a good environment for the children and the vandalisation is costing the school money that they want to spend on other things.

PC Becker is the local policeman who is trying to make sure that the school is kept safe and who wants to catch the people who are causing so much trouble to the area.

A group of young people keep shoplifting in the local corner shop.

Mrs George works in the shop and keeps being blamed by the owners for not catching who is stealing from them.

Mr and Mrs Shilling own the shop and have worked hard to get it well established and making money as they are supporting their two daughters who are at University. They are thinking of closing the shop.

Bob, Shane and Raj plus a few other teenagers are all part of a group that dares each other to steal from the shop. They think it is funny.

Dan, Mark and Digby all go to the shop on their way home from school. They don't like the fact that they are always being watched and feel like people think they are the thieves. They have now stopped going to the shop but have found another one down the road.

Ted Oliver is an elderly gentleman in his 90s. He has been visiting the corner shop here since he was a young boy and uses it every day as a way of talking and meeting people. Since his wife died he gets very lonely.

Mrs Webster is the owner of 'Shop Video', a business that sells and then maintains shop video cameras. She has just been asked to install 4 cameras in the corner shop.

Compromise

SESSION OBJECTIVES

To understand that compromise is about finding a way to meet the needs of both people and not about giving in.

SESSION OUTCOMES

✓ To use a problem-solving approach to explore what people want or need and then find solutions to meet those needs.

LESSON PLAN

➢ Ask the children to think of a time when they have noticed that their baby needed something and that their parent put their own needs on hold to meet the baby's needs or found a way of them both having their needs met.

➢ Share and discuss what each person might have felt and why they behaved as they did.

For those classrooms not able to undertake the Circles for Learning Project, video clips or photographs can be used to support the discussion around the topic and stimulate thoughts and ideas from the children and young people.

Task

KS1: To be able to think about how the different characters feel and then generate lots of ideas about what could happen to solve their problem.

KS2/KS3: To work in small groups to generate ideas to solve a dilemma

KS1

1. Introduce the word 'compromise' and ask the children what they believe it means. Illustrate this by giving an example – two children in the playground who both want to ride the bike but there is only one bike.

2. Help the children to identify the problem – 'one bike and two children' – and then to find a solution – one child to go first and then the other.

   • One rides sitting on the saddle, the other goes on the back, standing on the metal that connects the wheels.
   • They go and play something else.

3. Show how there can be more than one solution and that the first part of solving the problem is to identify what the problem is and then generate ideas that may solve it. The third part is for both to suggest which solution they find acceptable and why.

4. Steps to success – use the diagram to highlight this to the children.

5. Read the story 'The Day No One Played Together' by Donalisa Helsley or 'Want to Play Trucks?' by Ann Stott and ask the children to spot the problem. Generate a solution as a class before you read how the children in the books handled things.

6. Place the steps to success in the classroom so that the children can see what they can do if they need to and then share and celebrate successful compromises.

KS2/KS3

1. Ask the children to work in pairs and discuss what the word 'compromise' means and to share an example.

2. Ask several of the pairs to share with the class.

3. Discuss what the children think about compromise – many will see compromise as someone having to give in. Suggest to the children that this isn't the case.

4. Share the Steps to Success diagram with the children and take an example to work through as a class:

   A brother and a sister are at home after school. Both have homework. Erin likes to work with her music on and Bobby likes quiet. Bobby has a really important science test the following day.

   • Define what the problem is
   • Generate solutions
   • Share which one they each prefer and say why
   • Create more solutions if needed
   • Agree on an outcome

5. Ask the children to work in small groups and explore the dilemmas. Each group will need to present to the class their dilemma and their solutions – the class will then divide into 2, one half playing one person, the other playing the second person. The class will then vote on which compromise is the one they are prepared to accept.

6. At the end, ask each person to say one thing they will take away from the lesson that has been useful, interesting or otherwise.

RESOURCES

1. *The Day No-one Played Together: A Story about Compromise* by Donalisa Helsley

2. *Want to Play Trucks?* by Ann Stott

3. Problem-solving sheet

4. Dilemma sheet

IMPORTANT POINTS

By listening to what another person is saying about an issue and then being creative with ideas, compromise can often be reached.

LEARNING LINKS

Emotional literacy, empathy, friendships, relationships, working together, self-awareness.

REFLECTION

Questions:

Positive comment from child:

Positive comment from adult:

LEARNING DIMENSIONS		SOCIAL & EMOTIONAL SKILLS	
Strategic awareness		Emotional literacy	🟩
Learning relationships	🟩	Neuroscience	
Curiosity		Self-regulation	
Creativity		Self-development	🟩
Meaning making			
Changing & learning	🟧		
Resilience	🟩		

Molly and her sister Sally are both going out to meet friends at different places. They both want to use the bathroom to wash their hair before they go. They both have to be ready at the same time as their Mum is dropping them off.	Sharif and Hector are good friends and live next to each other. Each week they go to Air Cadets together. They normally ride their bikes to cadets. Hector's bike has broken and he wants Sharif to walk. Sharif doesn't want to walk.
Rick and Steff have been paired to work on a project together. Rick likes bikes and football and Steff likes skateboards and ice hockey. They have to agree a project and complete an outline by the end of the week to hand in.	Sienna and Tegan have to do after school clubs until Tegan's Mum can pick them up after work. Tegan doesn't want to be on her own in a group and Sienna has agreed to stay with her. The clubs are Photography, Art, Chess, netball or gardening. Sienna enjoys art and Tegan enjoys being outside and physical things.
Alex and Dylan both go to an activity week over the summer. Alex's Mum takes them and Dylan's Mum picks them both up. As Dylan has never been before Alex has agreed to look out for him. Dylan and Alex have to choose their groups and Dylan wants Alex to go to tennis with him as one of his choices but this clashes with Karate, which is what Alex wants to do.	Priti and Stacey are both doing Art at school together. They have just been asked to choose a topic to explore and both want to do the same project – landscapes. The teacher has said that everyone needs to be different. The other projects are sea, space, city, rainforest or mountains.
Izzy and Syreeta are both doing science at school and have been paired up for the science project week. Izzy is really interested in environmental issues where as Syreeta is really interested in robotics. They can't agree on a topic to work with as they both feel very strongly about their area.	Shane and Raj are both in the school football team. Raj really enjoys being in goal and so does Shane the PE teacher has left them to decide who will be the goalie for the first game of the season against their arch rivals Heatherdowns School.

Success

Step 5

The two people agree on the solution and follow this.

Step 4

Check that the problem is still the same if not start again.

Step 3

Each person choose the idea that they like the most and say why

Step 2

Generate ideas that solve the problem

Step 1

Identify the problem

Problem solving

SESSION OBJECTIVES

To be able to listen and think about a problem and then generate ideas to solve the problem before exploring each one to find the right solution.

SESSION OUTCOMES

✓ To be able to generate ideas to solve a problem and then explore their consequences.

LESSON PLAN

➢ Ask the children to think of a time that they have watched their class parent solve a problem for their class baby. Ask them to describe the problem that the baby had, and the different ways the parent tried to solve this, how many different ways they tried before they found a good fit.

For those classrooms not able to undertake the Circles for Learning Project, video clips or photographs can be used to support the discussion around the topic and stimulate thoughts and ideas from the children and young people.

Task

KS1: To be able to identify the problem in a story and then think of solutions.

KS2: To be able to identify the problem in the animation and generate ideas to solve the problems.

KS3: To be able to explore the different layers of problems and generate ideas to solve them

KS1

1. Explain to the children that you need them to solve a problem. That they need to work together to generate ideas and then choose the best one to do the job.

2. They need to be the problem solvers.

3. Ask each child to draw themselves as a problem solver with a special costume.

4. Read the story *A Kiss for Giraffe* by Judith Koppens. Stop when the problem becomes clear and ask the children to work in groups and

- Define the problem
- Generate 3 solutions that could solve the problem

5. Ask each group to present their ideas to the class.

6. Write them on the board and then discuss them.

7. As a class, choose their top 3.

8. Complete the book and share the idea the author came up with.

KS2

1. Explain to the children that you need then to solve a problem. That they need to work together to generate ideas and then choose the best one to do the job.

2. They need to be the problem solvers.

3. Watch the short film 'Dust Buddies'.

4. Stop the film before the dust buddy starts to show how he will get his friend out of the hoover.

5. Ask the children to work in pairs and generate 3 solutions to the problem.

6. Ask the children to choose one solution and write the next part of the story.

7. Ask the children to share their stories.

8. Watch the end of 'Dust Buddies'.

9. What did they think?

KS3

1. Share the story with the children.

2. Ask them to work in pairs to record the different problems from the information.

3. Share the story *The Island* by Armin Greder with the children and then explore what the problems are at the different levels.

- A man has been washed up on the beach who is different – what should happen to him?
- Being different is not safe
- No one wants to welcome the stranger
- No one wants to be responsible for the stranger

- The foreigner is a savage – he eats with his hands and he eats bones. He could be dangerous
- Other savages may come to the island

The thinking that develops throughout the book shows how the problem changes:

- The man on the beach is different
- Different is bad
- Different that is bad could be dangerous
- Dangerous means no one is safe
- If no one is safe we have to defend ourselves
- The only way to keep us safe is to get rid of the danger
- The only way to get rid of the dangerous savage is to send him back out to sea and kill him
- The only way to protect ourselves from future danger is to build a wall

4. What are the different problems in the story?

5. Depending on what the problem is depends on what solution is needed.

6. Ask the children to work in pairs or small groups and explore together one of the problems identified and generate some possible solutions.

E.g. – A man has been washed up on the beach – PROBLEM

Solutions

- Take him in and look after him
- Send him back out to sea
- Lock him up
- Kill him

The man is different – PROBLEM

Solutions

- Welcome the difference and learn new things
- Fear difference and get rid of it
- Shut things that are different away so you don't have to think about it

No one wants to look after the stranger – PROBLEM

Solutions

- The leader can model how to behave and invite the stranger to his home
- The stranger can stay in an empty home

- The stranger can be asked to leave
- The stranger can be left alone

Which solution is chosen depends on how the stranger is thought about – how things are thought about depends on your experience and your culture/family/community

RESOURCES

1. YouTube clip: CGI Animated Short Film HD 'Dust Buddies' by Beth Tomashek & Sam Wade/ CGMeetup,
www.youtube.com/watch?v=mZ6eeAjgSZI&index=1&list=PLMizheSITLyBew_HdvvzzPFS3X7PBQRbL

2. Chunking sheet

3. Chunking definition

4. *A Kiss for Giraffe* by Judith Koppens

5. *The Island* by Armin Greder

IMPORTANT POINTS

How we think about things is a core component of how we problem solve. If we can think flexibly we are more likely to generate enough possible solutions to a problem.

LEARNING LINKS

Friendships, working together, self-awareness, problem solving.

REFLECTION

Questions:

Positive comment from child:

Positive comment from adult:

LEARNING DIMENSIONS		SOCIAL & EMOTIONAL SKILLS	
Strategic awareness	■	Emotional literacy	
Learning relationships		Neuroscience	
Curiosity		Self-regulation	
Creativity	■	Self-development	■
Meaning making	■		
Changing & learning	■		
Resilience			

Recounting

SESSION OBJECTIVES

To be able to share a verbal description of an event including what happened, feelings and actions.

SESSION OUTCOMES

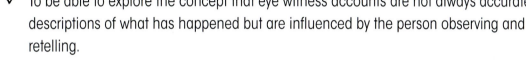

✓ To be able to share a verbal account of an event.

✓ To be able to explore the concept that eye witness accounts are not always accurate descriptions of what has happened but are influenced by the person observing and retelling.

LESSON PLAN

➤ Ask the children to recall a time when their class parent was telling them about something their class baby had done. How is their description different from one that an observer might describe?

For those classrooms not able to undertake the Circles for Learning Project, video clips or photographs can be used to support the discussion around the topic and stimulate thoughts and ideas from the children and young people.

Task

KS1: To be able to verbally share an event that they observed or took part in and share what happened and how they felt.

KS2: To be able to explore eye witness accounts and understand that they are not always accurate but are influenced by the interpretations of the observer.

KS3: To research information on eye witness accounts and their reliability

KS1

1. Ask the children to tell you about an event that they have watched – an assembly, a school performance or an event.

2. Let them take it in turns and list what happened on the board to show the sequence of events.

3. Introduce the word 'sequence' and explore this with the children.

4. Ask the children to work in groups and give them a story sequence – either pictures or words – and ask them to put it in the correct order.

5. Share what each group has created.

6. Then ask the groups to put the sequence in a different order and create a different story.

7. Share the stories with the class.

KS2

1. Explain to the children you are going to show them a short clip and then you would like them to tell you what happened, to describe it as well as they can.

2. Share the 'Test Your Awareness – Whodunnit?' video clip

3. Ask the children to talk you through what happened and write the sequence on the board.

4. Ask the children to get into groups of 4 and explain that you have a quiz for them.

   Questions:
   • What was in the maid's hand?
   • What was on the floor next to the body?
   • What was behind the maid?
   • What was the picture on the wall?
   • What were the flowers on the table – roses or lilies?
   • What was on the wall behind the policeman?
   • Who was wearing a hat?
   • What was the butler holding?
   • Who was wearing glasses?
   • What colour was the detective's coat?

5. Did anyone notice the changes made in the film?

6. Watch again and see what you notice.

7. Discuss the accuracy of an eye witness account.

8. Share the Venn diagram and explain that there is often information that is shared by both people; however, each person also has their own version of the story.

9. Remind them of the work on points of view and the book *The Tale of Two Beasts* by Fiona Roberton.

10. Explore how this information might help with arguments between people.

KS3

1. Pose the question – How reliable is an eyewitness account? Put the statement 'An eyewitness account is very reliable' at one end of the line and 'An eyewitness is not very reliable' at the other end of the line, creating a spectrum. Ask the children to stand on the line showing what they believe.

2. Ask the children to work in pairs and research what they can find on eyewitness accounts.

3. Ask each pair to share a 3 minute presentation in a form they would like to the other children about what they have found. They could use a video to illustrate their point or a game.

4. Share the presentations and discuss what they have found. How surprised are they? How will this new knowledge impact on their life? You could introduce the Venn diagram and help them explore what happens when people argue over things. They are likely to remember different things as different things are important to different people.

5. Share a newspaper article sharing an eye witness account and discuss how this has been used.

6. Share with the children the 'Monkey Business' video clip and the eyewitness inaccuracy if children have not found this information in their research.

RESOURCES

1. Newspaper article sharing eye witness accounts of an incident

2. 'The monkey business illusion'
   www.youtube.com/watch?v=IGQmdoK_ZfY

3. 'Brain games – eyewitness inaccuracy, source monitoring error, and misinformation effect',
   www.youtube.com/watch?v=RWO2UQ4MW7U

4. 'Test Your Awareness – Whodunnit?'
   www.youtube.com/watch?v=ubNF9QNEQLA

5. *The Tale of Two Beasts* by Fiona Roberton

IMPORTANT POINTS

Being able to give a verbal recount of an event is linked to sharing what happened in the right order so that it is coherent. It needs to be remembered that our eye witness statement is influenced by our own beliefs and is not always accurate. It is our perception of an event.

LEARNING LINKS

Working together, teamwork, friendships.

REFLECTION

Questions:

Positive comment from child:

Positive comment from adult:

LEARNING DIMENSIONS		SOCIAL & EMOTIONAL SKILLS	
Strategic awareness	🟩	Emotional literacy	
Learning relationships	🟧	Neuroscience	
Curiosity		Self-regulation	
Creativity		Self-development	🟩
Meaning making	🟩		
Changing & learning			
Resilience			

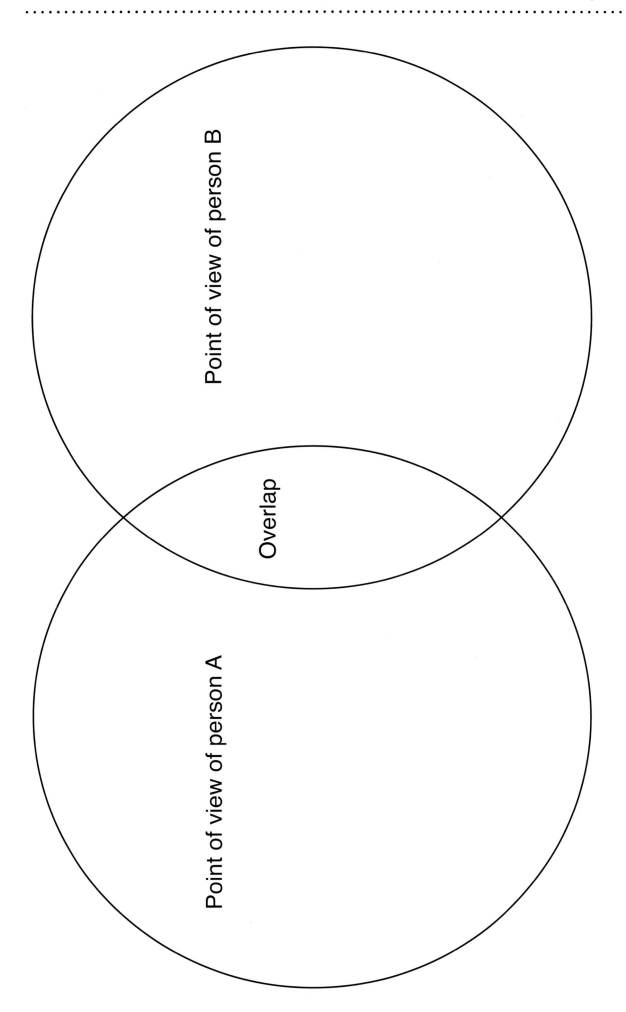

The mean hungry wolf ran to her Grandma's house. He was going to hide and wait for her. He wanted to eat her up.

The big bad wolf locked Grandma in a cupboard.

Little Red Riding Hood was sent into the forest to take her Grandma something to eat as she had been unwell.

The big bad wolf put on Grandma's bed hat and climbed into bed and waited for Little Red Riding Hood.

A woodcutter heard a girl crying for help and ran to her rescue.

Little Red Riding Hood ran out of the cottage . 'Help me, help me.' she cried.

A mean hungry wolf watched her as she skipped through the woods to her Grandma's house.

The woodcutter killed the big bad wolf and saved Little Red Riding Hood and her Grandma.

Little Red Riding Hood arrived. She noticed that her Grandma looked very different.

Little Red Riding Hood asked Grandma why her teeth were so big. The big bad wolf jumped out of bed and tried to eat her with his shiny white teeth.

One day Mummy Pig called her three babies to her and told them it was time for them to leave home and build a house of their own.

The little pigs lit the fire in their house of bricks.

The three little pigs found some straw, some sticks and some bricks.

The three little pigs built a house of straw. The big bad wolf came along and asked to be let in. The pigs said no.

The wolf huffed and puffed and blew their house down. The pigs ran away.

The big bad wolf fell into the fire and died.

The pigs made their second house out of strong twigs.

The wolf came along and asked to be let in. The three little pigs said no. The wolf huffed and puffed and blew down their house of twigs.

The pigs built a house of bricks. The big bad wolf came along and asked to be let in. They said no. He huffed and puffed and couldn't blow their house down.

The big bad wolf went onto the roof and climbed down the chimney.

The baby pigs were very excited and went out to find the things to build a house with.

A big brown fox walked by and saw the gingerbread man. 'Can I help you?' he asked.	The little old lady made some ginger-bread and cut out a gingerbread man.
The gingerbread man asked the fox to carry him over the river. The fox let the ginger-bread man jump onto his head.	She put the ginger-bread man in the oven to cook.
The fox loved to eat gingerbread men.	The gingerbread man jumped out of the oven and ran away. As he ran he sang 'You can't catch me I'm the gingerbread man.'
As the fox swam with the gingerbread man on his head, he flipped him up and opened his mouth and ate him.	The little old lady, the little old man, the dog and the pig ran after the gingerbread man.
	The gingerbread man ran and ran until he came to a river. He couldn't swim.

Persistence

SESSION OBJECTIVES

To understand that persistence is a trait that means we are motivated to keep trying to achieve a goal and that setbacks are overcome.

SESSION OUTCOMES

✓ To explore what kept us going when the going got tough and what stopped us giving up.

LESSON PLAN

➢ Ask the children to remember a time when they watched their class baby persist at something despite several setbacks. What kept them going?

For those classrooms not able to undertake the Circles for Learning Project, video clips or photographs can be used to support the discussion around the topic and stimulate thoughts and ideas from the children and young people.

Task

KS1: To create a picture to show the hardest thing they have learnt to do and to show what enabled them to keep going.

KS2: To create an acrostic poem to motivate themselves when they need to keep going.

KS3: Create a motivational video.

KS1

1. Ask the children to share

    • Something they have learnt today
    • Something they have learnt to do recently
    • The hardest thing they have learnt to do

2. Make sure that the adults join in with this.

3. Explore the hardest thing they children feel they have learnt to do. Why was it hard? Why did they keep going? Who helped them keep going? What was the self-talk in their head?

4. Introduce the word 'persistence' and explain this word to the children.

5. Point out persistence in the classroom over the next few weeks; model it with the work the adults are doing.

6. Ask them to draw a picture of them learning to do something and then to draw

    •   One person who helped them
    •   The self-talk that got them through

7. Share the pictures and make a display about learning and what keeps us going when the going gets tough.

8. Share the book *Everyone Can Learn to Ride a Bicycle* by Chris Raschka.

KS2

1. Share the video – 'Real stories proving you should never give up'.

2. Ask the children to work in pairs and to interview each other and find out the answers to the questions:

    •   Why did the mum give the boy a puppy?
    •   What enabled the puppy to keep trying? What was the self-talk in his head like?
    •   What made the boy change his mind and play with the puppy?
    •   What is a good word to describe the puppy's ability to keep going when it got tough?
    •   What is something that you have kept going with even though it was difficult and you kept getting it wrong?
    •   What enabled you to keep going?
    •   Who helped you when it got tough?
    •   What did they do that helped?
    •   What was the self-talk that you heard in your head? Was it positive or negative?

3. Ask each child to present to the class the interview that they undertook with their partner.

4. Make a list of the people who helped the children, what enabled them to keep going and the positive self-talk that they used.

5. Ask the children to take a phrase used as self-talk or that someone has said which they like and think is powerful and create an acrostic poem to give them the motivation to keep going when they meet another tough issue.

    Y – You have the courage to keep going
    O – One step at a time
    U – Up one rung at a time right to the end and success

C – Count to 10 and go again

A – Ask for help to keep you going

N – No negative self-talk allowed

D – Don't give up

O – One way to go – to the top

I – If you need to call a friend do it

T – Talk yourself through it – go for gold

KS3

1. Share with the children a motivational video 'Resilient Best Motivation Video'

2. Discuss what it includes:

   - Good music builds to a finale
   - A key phrase
   - Use of voice – loud and fast to make things stand out
   - Use of language
   - Use of positive pictures with people working hard and achieving
   - The use of a metaphor to help create a story

3. Set the challenge: – As a group, create your own motivational video or individually create your own motivational mood board.

   The mood board needs to contain

   - A piece of music that inspires you
   - A picture that motivates you
   - A phrase that makes you feel good
   - A film that makes you feel good
   - A story of a time when you triumphed over something
   - A picture of you achieving something you wanted
   - Someone who inspires you
   - Someone who you hold as a role model
   - An object that is important to you
   - A goal that you want to achieve

4. Create a class exhibition and show the work the children have created or ask each child to present their video or motivational mood board.

RESOURCES

1. 'Real stories proving you should never give up',
   www.youtube.com/watch?v=ILcGPGteSGg

2. *Everyone Can Learn to Ride a Bicycle* by Chris Raschka

3. 'Resilient – best motivation video',
   www.youtube.com/watch?v=PdjHG_bGKhk&pbjreload=10

4. Tablet computers

IMPORTANT POINTS

Persistence is a trait that keeps us going when things get tough. It is also known as 'grit'.

LEARNING LINKS

Self-awareness, motivation, emotional literacy.

REFLECTION

Questions:

Positive comment from child:

Positive comment from adult:

LEARNING DIMENSIONS		SOCIAL & EMOTIONAL SKILLS	
Strategic awareness		Emotional literacy	
Learning relationships		Neuroscience	
Curiosity		Self-regulation	
Creativity		Self-development	
Meaning making			
Changing & learning			
Resilience			

Chapter 6

Team building and collaboration

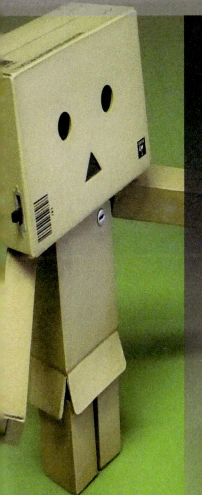

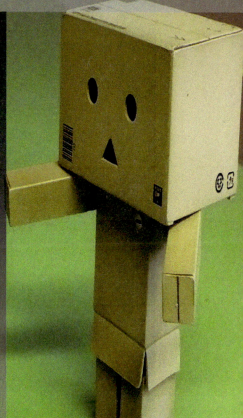

RESPECT   193

ENCOURAGEMENT   198

ACCEPTING THE OPINIONS
AND IDEAS OF OTHERS   202

FLEXIBILITY   206

CONSTRUCTIVE FEEDBACK   211

PROBLEM SOLVING   217

SUPPORTING OTHERS   221

Respect

SESSION OBJECTIVES

To be able to share what the word 'respect' means and to give examples of what would be respectful and what would be disrespectful.

SESSION OUTCOMES

✓ To be able to explain what respectful behaviours, attitudes and ways of being are and why they are important.

LESSON PLAN

➢ Ask the children to remember a time when their class parent shared with them how difficult it can be to be a parent. Explore with the children what might happen if two parents had different views on how to do something.

➢ Ask the children to decide on questions that they could ask their class parent that might explore what they did if they didn't agree with their partner.

For those classrooms not able to undertake the Circles for Learning Project, video clips or photographs can be used to support the discussion around the topic and stimulate thoughts and ideas from the children and young people.

Task

KS1: To create a class acrostic poem showing what 'respect' means in their class.

KS2: To be able to list what respectful behaviours attitudes and ways of being are and also what disrespectful behaviours, attitudes or ways of being are.

KS3: To create a montage illustrating what respect means.

KS1

1. Read *I Don't Care: Learning about Respect* by Brian Moses with the children and discuss what respect means.

2. Working in pairs, ask the children to come up with a definition.

3. Share the definitions children have come up with.

4. Lay them out on the floor and ask the children to stand next to the one they feel defines the word best. Take away the least popular definition and ask the children to stand by the one they feel describes the word again. Continue doing this until you have the top 3 definitions.

5. Share with the children that you are going to create a class acrostic poem for the word 'respect' and the word 'disrespect'.

6. Ask the children to work in pairs and come up with a sentence for each of the letters in the word 'respect'.

7. Share the ones the children have come up with, Write them on strips of paper and lay them on the tables.

8. Give each child a sticky note and ask them to write their name on it. Then ask them to put their note on the sentence they like the best for the letter R.

9. Choose the most popular sentence for the poem.

10. Do the same with the other letters.

11. Give a sentence to 7 of the pairs and ask them to write it out and decorate it.

12. Share the word 'disrespect' with the children and ask them to come up with a definition.

13. Share the definition and choose the one that they believe is the best by asking them to stand by it, as you did with the 'respect' definition.

14. Once you have your definition, share out the letters to the working pairs and ask them to come up with a sentence for their letter that illustrates disrespectful behaviour or attitudes.

15. Once all the letters have a sentence, ask the children to write and decorate their sentence and then create the two poems – one showing RESPECT and the other showing DISRESPECT.

KS2

1. Write the work 'respect' on the board and then ask the children to work in pairs to come up with

- A definition
- A picture showing respect
- A poem or a song about respect
- A quote about respecting others
- A quote about self-respect

2. Ask the children to lay out their collection on the table and then ask the pairs to walk around and undertake a silent exhibition.

3. Discuss what they have seen and what this has made them think about.

4. Ask the children to create a list showing disrespectful attitudes and behaviours and respectful attitudes and behaviour. They can do this in a variety of ways:

    *   A list
    *   A series of pictures
    *   A table
    *   A Mind Map®

5. Share the different ways children have chosen to record their ideas and what they have come up with.

6. After they have seen the different things that people have found and shared in their list, ask them how RESPECT should be taught – both at home and in school.

KS3

1. Share a RESPECT word cloud with the children and discuss what it shows

2. Ask them to work in pairs and define the words RESPECT and DISRESPECT.

3. Working in pairs, ask them to create a montage for RESPECT and DISRESPECT.
    This needs to be made up of words, pictures, quotes, sayings, songs, poems etc.

4. When the children have finished, create an exhibition to share their work.

5. Discuss what they have learnt from the task.

    1. What have they found out that is important to them?
    2. What have they learnt?
    3. How will this impact on their behaviour in the future?
    4. How will they challenge disrespectful behaviour in the future?
    5. How will they promote respectful behaviour?
    6. What one thing could the class do that would promote respectful behaviour?

RESOURCES

1. *I Don't Care: Learning about Respect* by Brian Moses

2. Internet access

3.   Large paper

4.   Pens

5.   Crayons/felt tips

IMPORTANT POINTS

'Respect' means to treat everything with care and consideration and to value difference.

LEARNING LINKS

Self-discovery, teamwork, emotional literacy, citizenship.

REFLECTION

Questions:

Positive comment from child:

Positive comment from adult:

LEARNING DIMENSIONS		SOCIAL & EMOTIONAL SKILLS	
Strategic awareness	🟧	Emotional literacy	
Learning relationships		Neuroscience	
Curiosity		Self-regulation	
Creativity	🟩	Self-development	🟩
Meaning making	🟧		
Changing & learning	🟩		
Resilience			

R
E
S
P
E
C
T

Encouragement

SESSION OBJECTIVES

To be able to understand the importance of encouragement and how it makes us feel. To be able to develop the skills of encouraging others.

SESSION OUTCOMES

✓ To be able to share how encouragement has made a difference to them and ways that they could encourage others.

LESSON PLAN

➢ Ask the children to share a time when they have observed their class parent encourage their class baby.

➢ Reflect on how that makes the baby feel and how that will impact on the way they experience the world in the future.

For those classrooms not able to undertake the Circles for Learning Project, video clips or photographs can be used to support the discussion around the topic and stimulate thoughts and ideas from the children and young people.

Task

KS1: To create a team poster to show ways of encouraging others.

KS2: To create a short sketch to illustrate the power of encouragement both in the present and how that experience may impact on a person's future.

KS3: To explore through debate whether it is good to encourage your children.

KS1

1. Share a picture of a parent encouraging a child to ride a bike.

2. Ask the children to describe what they can see.

3. Highlight the word 'encouragement' when it comes up.

4. Ask the children to define this word and then share a time when they experienced it.

5. Give each child a square of paper (15cm works well) and ask them to draw a picture of a time when someone encouraged them to do something. Give them a sticky note speech bubble and ask them to write on it what the words were that this person used.

6. Create a montage to show all the different ways that the children have been encouraged to do things and the words that others have used. A bit like a patchwork quilt.

7. Ask the children to make an 'Encouragement Creature' out of modelling clay that they can give to each other as a way of showing encouragement.

KS2

1. Share the video clip 'One Small Step'.

2. Create a line to show a spectrum with 'It is important for parents to encourage their children' one end and 'Parents shouldn't encourage their children' the other.

3. Ask the children to stand on the line to show what they believe.

4. Ask each child to share their reason for where they stand.

5. When everyone has finished, give the children the option of moving if they like.

6. Ask the children to work in small groups and to create a sketch to show how encouragement can affect someone's future – this may be in a good or a bad way. Parents who overly encourage may cause children to hate something and refuse to do it. Too little encouragement may give children a message that nothing is important.

7. Share the different sketches and discuss what the children have learnt. How will this impact on their future?

KS3

1. Share the video clip 'One Small Step'.

2. Create a line to show a spectrum with 'It is important for parents to encourage their children' one end and 'Parents shouldn't encourage their children' the other.

3. Ask the children to stand on the line to show what they believe.

4. Ask each child to share their reason for where they stand.

5. When everyone has finished, give the children the option of moving if they like.

6. Ask the class to divide into two teams – those who will argue that encouragement is positive to development and those who will argue that encouragement is bad for development

7. Give each team time to research and come up with arguments to support their statement.

8. Set out the seating so both teams face each other.

9. Ensure that the teams understand that only one person can talk at a time and that if they wish to talk they need to stand up. Once one person has finished talking, they can choose the next person but they have to be on the opposing team.

10. After half the time, ask if people would like to change teams.

11. Allow this option.

12. Continue the debate.

13. Once the debate is finished, ask the children:

    •   What did you learn that was new?
    •   What is a thought you would like to explore?
    •   How will you try to be as a parent?
    •   What is a way that we as a class can encourage you?
    •   What can you do to encourage yourself?

RESOURCES

1. Animated short film: 'One Small Step', www.youtube.com/watch?v=yWd4mzGqQYo

2. Modelling clay

IMPORTANT POINTS

Encouragement is a very powerful action and can cause people to thrive and get better or to get angry and stop.

LEARNING LINKS

Friendships, emotional literacy, teamwork, sense of self, working with others.

REFLECTION

Questions:

Positive comment from child:

Positive comment from adult:

LEARNING DIMENSIONS		SOCIAL & EMOTIONAL SKILLS	
Strategic awareness	🟧	Emotional literacy	
Learning relationships		Neuroscience	
Curiosity		Self-regulation	
Creativity	🟩	Self-development	🟩
Meaning making	🟧		
Changing & learning	🟩		
Resilience			

Accepting the opinions and ideas of others

SESSION OBJECTIVES

To be able to work within a group and create a group ethos which shows that all ideas are welcome and will be thought about.

SESSION OUTCOMES

✓ To demonstrate how ideas and thoughts can be accepted and welcomed into work or play.

LESSON PLAN

➢ Ask the children to share a time when they watched their class parent accept an idea or way of doing something that their class baby did, despite knowing it wouldn't work.

➢ Explore with the group why this might be a positive way of being and what the baby might learn from this.

For those classrooms not able to undertake the Circles for Learning Project, video clips or photographs can be used to support the discussion around the topic and stimulate thoughts and ideas from the children and young people.

Task

KS1: Create a puppet show to demonstrate how to accept another person's idea.

KS2/KS3: Undertake a team challenge demonstrating how everyone's ideas can be accepted and thought about.

KS1

1. Share with the children a puppet show demonstrating one puppet suggesting an idea to another. Demonstrate how not to accept another person's idea: laugh, make fun of their idea, pull it apart and say why it won't work, tell them they are not good at this sort of thing etc.

2. Ask the children what they thought about the way the idea was received.

3. Tease out the points that they noticed and write them on the board and then get children to work out the opposite way of dealing with an idea given.

    Made fun of the idea – Take all ideas seriously; people have worked hard at thinking about them. That won't work because . . . That is an interesting idea. Help me understand how that might work.

4. Divide the children into small groups and ask them to create a puppet show to share how an idea or a suggestion could be received.

5. Share the different puppet shows and discuss the points each one demonstrated.

6. Ask the children what the most important aspect of learning was for them from the work they have done.

7. Ask the children to share one thing they are going to try and do in the future.

KS2/KS3

1. Demonstrate to the children ways that ideas can be received.

2. Ask them to give a thumbs up if they think it is a positive way or a thumbs down if they think it is negative.

3. Discuss the impact of both negative and positive ways of having your idea received: it makes you feel like part of the team, it makes you want to support and share your ideas OR it makes you feel like no one thinks your ideas are worth anything, makes you not want to join in and share ideas.

4. Explain to the children that you are going to set them a team challenge and you want them to practise accepting ideas in a positive way.

5. As they work on their challenge, they are going to be observed by 2 observers whose job it is to count how many different ways they accept ideas as a team.

6. Set the challenge and then give the children 10 minutes to work out different phrases or ways of receiving ideas in their group before they start the challenge and the observers start to watch.

7. Ask the observers to write down the best responses that they hear to share with everyone later.

    The challenge is to make a Lego® puzzle square – see diagram. (This is a bit like a 3D tangram.)

8. Share the best responses to ideas that the observers heard.

9. Ask the children to share how it felt when they heard an idea from someone else. And then how the person felt when their idea was welcomed.

RESOURCES

1. Puppets

2. Team challenge

3. Postcards with sayings on them

4. Lego puzzle ideas

IMPORTANT POINTS

Being open to new ideas enables creativity and problem solving to become stronger.

LEARNING LINKS

Teamwork, emotional literacy, self-development, problem solving, friendships.

REFLECTION

Questions:

Positive comment from child:

Positive comment from adult:

LEARNING DIMENSIONS		SOCIAL & EMOTIONAL SKILLS	
Strategic awareness	🟧	Emotional literacy	
Learning relationships		Neuroscience	
Curiosity		Self-regulation	
Creativity	🟩	Self-development	🟩
Meaning making	🟧		
Changing & learning	🟩		
Resilience			

Flexibility

SESSION OBJECTIVES

To explore the concept of flexibility and how having flexible thinking can be a positive trait.

SESSION OUTCOMES

✓ To explore what the word flexible means and then to demonstrate flexible thinking, sharing why this might be a useful trait to have.

LESSON PLAN

➢ Ask the children to share a time when they watched their class parent be flexible in their thinking about their class baby. This might be while they were doing something together, getting the baby to do what they wanted, encouraging them to do something they didn't want to do, eating new things etc.

For those classrooms not able to undertake the Circles for Learning Project, video clips or photographs can be used to support the discussion around the topic and stimulate thoughts and ideas from the children and young people.

Task

KS1: To look at the properties of flexible and non-flexible things and why they are suitable for different things.

KS2: To create something new from something old.

KS3: To work in groups and explore the saying 'If you always do what you have always done then you'll always get what you have always got.' To explore cognitive flexibility scenarios.

KS1

1. Share a range of materials with the children and ask them to describe their properties. Pipe cleaner, plastic ruler, pencil, metal ruler, plastic cup, china mug, rubber hose etc.

2. Make links to the fact that the materials' properties suit the role that they are doing – a cup handle made of a pipe cleaner wouldn't be very useful!!

3. Create some silly things together – a pencil made of a rubber hose would be quite difficult to write with. A cup made from metal would be very hot to hold.

4. Introduce the concept of flexible thinking and ask the children what they think that might be.

5. Can they identify times when this might be useful? – when two people have argued and are trying to find a solution or when something doesn't work and you are trying to find another way of doing something etc.

6. Explore the opposite of flexible thinking – rigid thinking.

7. When might rigid thinking be useful? – when something has to be done in a certain way or when you have to stick to the rules.

8. Watch the *Sesame Street* clip 'Grover and Zachary Quinto are Flexible'.

9. Collect different examples of flexible and rigid thinking in class and make a display.

KS2

1. Watch the video animation Treasure

2. Discuss how the old lady was able to make something out of nothing and how much pleasure it gave her.

3. Ask the children to work in pairs and identify three skills the old lady demonstrated – Creativity, imagination, flexible thinking, gratitude, curiosity, excitement etc

4. Ask the children to find 3 photos of recycled things that they like.

5. Lay the photos on the tables and allow the children to walk around and look at them. Discuss what they have found. If you have any recycled items, share these with the children.

6. Then ask the children to bring objects to school that are 'junk' and can be recycled. Explain that over the week you will all be collecting things to enable 'The Challenge' to happen the following week. The challenge is for each person to create a 'recycled gift' which will be displayed at a recycled exhibition.

7. Explore with the children flexible thinking – being able to change one thing into another. When would this type of thinking be useful?

8. Watch the YouTube clip 'Flexibility and accepting input from others in play'.

9. Discuss times when children have been able to do this and times when it has been really hard to be flexible.

10. Create the time to make the recycled gifts and discuss what the children have created and why. Take photos of the children as they work so that the journey is recorded. The first photo might be a pile of stuff, the second an object and the final one the end product.

11. Using the created gifts, organise an exhibition to show what the children have created.

12. Collect examples of flexible thinking both in and out of the classroom with the children and adults.

KS3

1. Watch the YouTube video clip 'How can I be more creative? Exercise cognitive flexibility with a mini creative thinking workshop'.

2. Discuss cognitive flexibility with the children. What have they learnt from this video clip? What has it made them think about? Ask children to share examples of times when they have seen things differently to another person.

3. Ask the groups to work in pairs explore the saying 'If you always do what you've always done you will always get what you have always got.' What does this mean? Can they give an example? Can they share a time when they tried something new and got a different response or outcome?

4. Share the story *The Island* by Armin Greder with the children. Discuss how the man on the beach might have felt, how the islanders felt and how the fisherman felt.

5. Divide the children into groups of 4. Ask the children to take on one of the characters and for the 4th person to be the interviewer.

6. Lay out chairs in a triangle with one character sitting on each chair.

7. The interviewer is able to move around the triangle and ask questions.

8. Once each person has answered their question they move seats and become another person.

9. Keep changing until all the questions have been asked.

10. Discuss what it was like changing character and trying to answer the questions and seeing or imagining things from the different point of view.

RESOURCES

1. Video animation: 'Treasure' by Chelsea Bartlett,
   www.youtube.com/watch?v=PjgxCZnzGLQ

2. A range of broken things and junk

3. 'Sesame Street: Grover and Zachary Quinto are flexible',
   www.youtube.com/watch?v=LTryB55xbbY&list=PL2IaUn5FkXCJhWCgMNjf0sQrgneVU41om

4. 'Flexibility and accepting input from others in play',
   www.youtube.com/watch?v=KW53r14o9UE

5. 'How can I be more creative? Exercise cognitive flexibility with a mini creative thinking workshop',
   www.youtube.com/watch?v=c3vOdKONMsA

6. *The Island* by Armin Greder

IMPORTANT POINTS

Being flexible can enable people to grow and change.

LEARNING LINKS

Self-development, teamwork, problem solving, emotional literacy, relationships.

REFLECTION

Questions:

Positive comment from child:

Positive comment from adult:

LEARNING DIMENSIONS		SOCIAL & EMOTIONAL SKILLS	
Strategic awareness	🟧	Emotional literacy	
Learning relationships		Neuroscience	
Curiosity		Self-regulation	
Creativity	🟩	Self-development	🟩
Meaning making	🟧		
Changing & learning	🟩		
Resilience			

The man on the beach
The islanders
The fisherman
The interviewer

Questions

The man: How did you feel when you landed on the beach safely after your ship was destroyed?

The islanders: How did you feel when you saw the strange man on your beach?

The fisherman: What do you think it was like for the strange man on his small raft at sea?

The man: Were you worried when you saw the islanders come down onto the beach?

The islanders: What do you think the man on the beach wanted from you and your people?

The fisherman: Why did you argue with the islanders for them not to send the man back out to sea?

The man: How did it make you feel when the islanders took you to a deserted part of the island? What did you think would happen?

The islanders: Why did you lock the man on the beach up in the goat pen? What did you think he would do to you?

The fisherman: Why did you stand up for the man? How did it feel knowing all the other islanders didn't want him there?

The man: Why do you think the islanders were so frightened of you?

The islanders: What made you finally decide that the man had to go?

The fisherman: How did it feel to watch your fellow islanders treat the man as they did?

The man: Were you glad to leave the island in the end?

The islanders: How did it feel when the man finally went?

The fisherman: How did it feel to know that our fellow islanders didn't like you anymore because of the fact that you stood up for the strange man?

Constructive feedback

SESSION OBJECTIVES

To explore the skills needed to give constructive feedback to peers and to understand the impact this can have on learning.

SESSION OUTCOMES

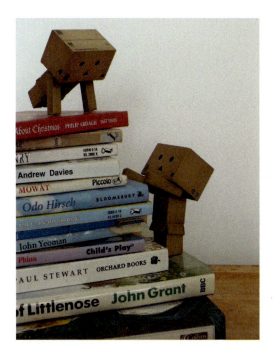

✓ To be able to give constructive feedback to another child, allowing them to build on the work they have already done and leaving them with a feeling of encouragement and not feeling as though they have failed.

LESSON PLAN

➤ Remind the children of a time when they observed their class parent teaching their class baby to do something. Explore with the children how this experience with their parent impacted on the child's later ability to learn in school.

➤ What messages would they like their class baby to receive about learning and how might these be given?

For those classrooms not able to undertake the Circles for Learning Project, video clips or photographs can be used to support the discussion around the topic and stimulate thoughts and ideas from the children and young people.

Task

KS1: Create a puppet show to demonstrate how to give constructive feedback to others.

KS2: Create a short sketch on how to give constructive feedback and enable someone to extend what they can do. OR a sketch that shows how not to give feedback and causes someone to feel as though they have failed. The focus is on the use of language – demonstrating the power of language.

KS3: Creating an advert for a course about how to give constructive feedback using non-judgmental language.

Team building and collaboration

KS1

1. Share something with the children that you are learning to do – playing an instrument, learning to dance, practising yoga or painting. Share how it feels when you can't get it right.

2. Ask them what they could say that might help you.

3. What is the purpose of their words? – To help you get better.

4. Write down the answers they give.

5. How can some feedback make you feel?

6. Go through the list and pull out the best things.

7. Think about how you might give feedback to someone else – can they come up with step by step instructions?

   - Ask how the person thinks they are doing
   - What are they pleased with?
   - What would they like help with? Be specific – I really need help in drawing heads on my people. I am happy with their arms and legs but the head is all wrong.
   - Look for what they are doing well with the head – the nose is really good but I think the head shape is not right; let's look at shapes of heads.
   - Remember, when you do things you need to do them a couple of times before they will be right.

8. Ask the children to work in pairs and create a puppet show or a short sketch that demonstrates how to give someone feedback so they can get better at something.

KS2

1. Ask the children to share what it is like to receive feedback on something that they have been working on.

2. Explore some of the language that can be used and put it in a Positive Use of Language or a Negative Use of Language column:

   - I really like the way you have used your pencil and shading to show the hair on your drawing.
   - The way you have drawn the eyes isn't very good.
   - The mouth is all wrong.
   - The hands of your person are a little out of proportion to the rest of the body.
   - You might like to have a look how the leg is made up – the muscles at the top and how they become the knee.

3.   Watch the YouTube clip – 'Giving and Receiving feedback' and 'Quick teaching tip: Feedback'.

4.   Discuss the two clips.

5.   Ask the children to work in pairs and create a short sketch that shows giving feedback in a very destructive way; then ring a bell and ask them to switch to giving feedback in a positive way; ring the bell again and ask them to switch – do this a couple of times for each group.

6.   Share the two sketches and ask the children to pick their favourite positive phrase. Collect these on the board and put them around the classroom.

7.   Ask the children to create Positive Feedback bookmarks with their 5 top tips.

KS3

1.   Introduce the concept of non-judgmental language.

That won't work OR Help me understand how that might work

2.   Discuss how the different uses of language can make people feel.

3.   Explore the reason for giving feedback to someone – to help them achieve or be able to do something better.

4.   Ask the children to work in small groups and give them the non-judgmental language game cut up and ask them to match up the phrases – positive non-judgmental and negative judgmental.

5.   Discuss what they have found and what they think of the language.

6.   Watch the YouTube clips on feedback.

7.   Discuss the way the clip advertises the feedback course:

   •   Highlight the use of examples
   •   The use of positive language
   •   The way the video 'sells' the course to you and makes you feel that you need it.

8.   Ask the children to work in groups to come up with an advert for television that is promoting a course for teachers on how to give feedback to students.

9.   Share the different sketches with each other.

RESOURCES

1. 'Giving and receiving feedback – course trailer',

    www.youtube.com/watch?v=Qg7jZVJuDE0

2. 'Quick teaching tip: Feedback',

    www.youtube.com/watch?v=SYXgMobMU8U

3. Non-judgmental language match-up game

IMPORTANT POINTS

Giving feedback is about developing and extending the learner's ability.

LEARNING LINKS

Teamwork, friendships, self-development, skills for learning, emotional literacy.

REFLECTION

Questions:

Positive comment from child:

Positive comment from adult:

LEARNING DIMENSIONS		SOCIAL & EMOTIONAL SKILLS	
Strategic awareness	🟧	Emotional literacy	
Learning relationships		Neuroscience	
Curiosity		Self-regulation	
Creativity	🟩	Self-development	🟩
Meaning making	🟧		
Changing & learning	🟩		
Resilience			

NON-JUDGMENTAL LANGUAGE MATCH-UP	
That is ridiculous That is really unreasonable	I hadn't considered that, how will that work for both of us? Help me understand how that will work.
That doesn't make sense at all You're not making sense to me	I'm not following you . . . Help me understand what you mean. I don't understand, how will that work?
That's not workable That will never work	I'm not comfortable with that because . . . That's one option, however these are my concerns . . . I'd like to hear more about your thinking on how this might work.
You aren't doing this right You didn't do this right	This is different to what I expected. Does this way of doing it still meet the criteria?
We're not going anywhere If only you would stop . . . We'll never agree	It seems as though _____ may be getting in our way. I have no doubt we can find a solution. Let's look back at we have accomplished so far.
Why do you want X?	How did you get to X? What makes you want X? What makes X a good solution/choice?
Why did you do that?	What motivated you to do that? How did you get to that point? Share your thought processes in getting to that possible solution.
That has nothing to do with this	Talk me through your thinking? Share with me how you came to that conclusion.
The fact is . . . This is how it is:	Correct me if I'm wrong, I understand (state facts as you see them) . . . . The way I see it is . . .
I won't do X	I am not really comfortable doing X X makes me very nervous (etc.) because . . .
You haven't done X	I appreciate your willingness to do X . . . I am unsure why X hasn't been done, share your thinking?
You're wrong	My experience has been . . . I see this differently . . . I need to understand . . . better

Do X You should do X	I need help with X We need to get X done . . . what suggestions do you have? I'd like you to do X, will that work? Can you do X? Are you willing to do X?
I want X I must have X	One option I see is X . . . how does X work for you? One way I see to resolve this is X . . . what do you think of X? One option is X . . . X is important to me because . . .
We have nothing in common	We agree on . . . Let's explore what areas we believe are working well?
You're lying. I don't believe that.	I'm confused about . . . Help me understand. Can you share the thinking behind this?
You said . . . But you did . . .	Let me see if I have this right, you are saying . . . I'm not clear about . . . Let's focus on the future.
That's not fair	Let's find a solution that is fair for both of us. Let's explore this further so that we can both feel that we have achieved what we need.
You make me mad You're making me feel	I get upset when . . . I feel . . .
Yes, but . . .	Yes, and . . . Yes I can see your point, however . . . . . .

Problem solving

SESSION OBJECTIVES

To work as a team to solve a problem.

SESSION OUTCOMES

✓ To be able to support each person within the team and solve the team problem.

LESSON PLAN

➢ Ask the children to think of a time when their class parent has had to solve a problem that they have encountered linked to their class baby. This could have been how to get them to sleep, how to teach them to say please and thank you, how to get them to do something they didn't like.

➢ Explore the skills or traits that the parent would need to be able to do this successfully.

For those classrooms not able to undertake the Circles for Learning Project, video clips or photographs can be used to support the discussion around the topic and stimulate thoughts and ideas from the children and young people.

Task

KS1/KS2/KS3: To be able to get a member of their team through the maze.

KS1/KS2/KS3

1. Mark out a 4 x 4 grid on the floor with masking tape or in the playground with chalk. Each square needs to be about 50cm.

2. Using the grid sheets draw out a variety of paths across the grid – see example.

3. Ask the children to get into teams of 4–6.

4. Explain that the aim of the game is to work out the path across the grid and get to the other side.

5. Each team takes it in turns. Player 1 steps onto the grid and then moves to another square. If they get it right then the maze caller (an adult or another child) says nothing. If they get it wrong then a noise is made or a buzzer or bell is rung.

6. The next person from the team steps onto the grid (starting at the beginning) and has a go. No one from the team can talk but they can indicate or sign.

7. The second person continues to guess the way through the grid until the buzzer or bell ring. Once this happens, the next person steps onto the grid.

8. The game continues like this with each person having to start at the beginning until one of the team complete the path correctly.

RESOURCES

1. Masking tape to create a 4x4 square grid on the floor or chalk if outside on the playground. Each square needs to be 50cm

2. Paper grid

IMPORTANT POINTS

All ideas are important and people need to be encouraged if the team is to work successfully.

LEARNING LINKS

Teamwork, relationships, working together, friendships, skills for learning.

REFLECTION

Questions:

Positive comment from child:

Positive comment from adult:

LEARNING DIMENSIONS		SOCIAL & EMOTIONAL SKILLS	
Strategic awareness	🟧	Emotional literacy	
Learning relationships		Neuroscience	
Curiosity		Self-regulation	
Creativity	🟩	Self-development	🟩
Meaning making	🟧		
Changing & learning	🟩		
Resilience			

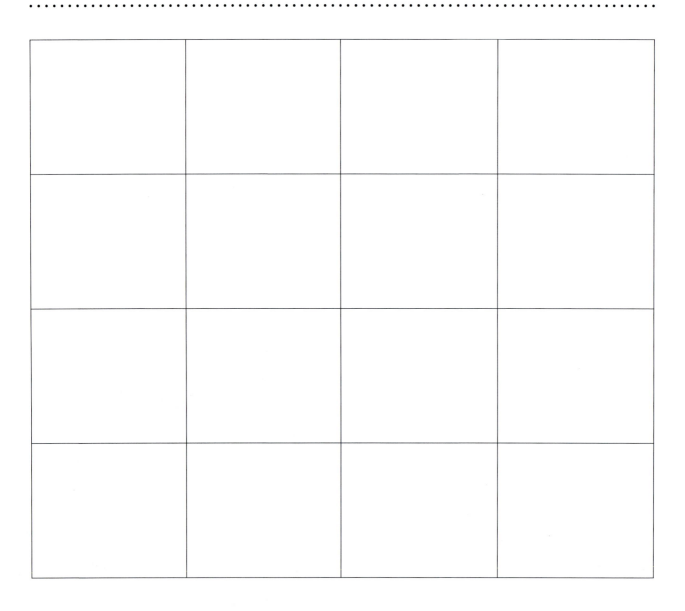

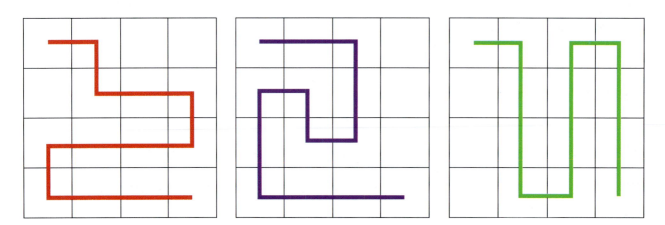

Examples of paths through the grid

Supporting others

SESSION OBJECTIVES

To support others in a variety of ways both in and out of the classroom.

SESSION OUTCOMES

✓ To be able to demonstrate and share a variety of ways to support others both in the classroom with learning and out of the classroom

LESSON PLAN

➢ Ask the children to think of ways that they have watched their class parent support their class baby.

➢ Explore how this might make the baby feel and how this may impact on the way they relate to others.

For those classrooms not able to undertake the Circles for Learning Project, video clips or photographs can be used to support the discussion around the topic and stimulate thoughts and ideas from the children and young people.

Task

KS1: Create a class assembly showing different ways to support others and how this can make people feel.

KS2: Maths problems workshop – children bring a maths puzzle to share and explain to others.

KS3: Beat that – a game where teams of children set a social dilemma for another team to work together to solve.

KS1

1. Share with the children a selection of photos showing people helping each other.

2. Ask the children what is special about the photos.

3. Discuss how the different people are feeling.

4. Link this to the story *Have You Filled a Bucket Today?* by Carol McCloud and David Messing. This shares the idea that when you help or support someone, it fills their bucket up, making them feel good but also fills your own up, meaning that when you help someone it makes you feel good.

5. Explain to the children that you have to create an assembly that shows why it is important to help others.

6. Divide the children up into small groups and ask them to come up with a short sketch that shows people helping or supporting others and shares how it makes people feel and why.

7. Share the different sketches and choose the ones that everyone feels shows why supporting others is good.

8. Help the children share their sketches but also explain how the different people feel in each one.

9. Put together a class assembly showing the sketches and explanations.

KS2

1. Divide the class into groups of 4–6 children and explain that for the next couple of weeks you are going to ask them to challenge each other, support each other and teach each other.

2. Create a timetable so that each group has a day over the next few weeks. Allocate one person to each week until all the children from each week have a day, e.g. Tom, Rick, Stan, Raj, Ben and Max are all in one group and their day is Monday. On Week 1, Raj presents, Week 2, Tom, Week 3, Rick, etc.

3. One person from each group needs to bring a maths challenge to share with the rest of their group on their week. This could be a puzzle, matchstick puzzle or number puzzle or word problem, etc.

4. Work with each group on each day (the presentation should take 30 minutes). Ask the person to share their maths challenge with the rest of their group. Give the group time to work on the challenge – they can ask questions about the challenge but the questions can only have a yes or no answer. Once the group has had time to work on the challenge people can say whether they have worked it out or not. Then ask the lead person to share how to work out their challenge with the group.

5. Explore the different ways we can support or help people in and around school – learning is only one way.

6. Ask the children to spot people being supportive to others and then share what they have seen at the end of the day.

KS3

1. Divide the children into groups of 4/5 and give them a photo and a name of a famous woman – ask them to find out who she is and what she did and then share this with the rest of the class.

2. Ask the children to present their famous woman and share what she did that makes her so special.

3. Explore why these people decided to help others in the way they did.

4. Ask each group to come up with 2 social dilemmas and give their dilemmas to another team. Each team has to discuss and problem solve to show what could be done. They need to be linked with how someone might help another person. For example:

    > Sam and Maddie come to school on the bus. They have a science test first lesson. The bus is running late so when they get to school they quickly get off and run to their lesson. Chaz has a Music exam first thing but as Chaz gets off the bus she realises that Sam or Maddie have left their Science book on the bus. What does she do? Ask the group to think of alternatives and then choose the one they feel is best.

5. Share the dilemmas so that each group has 2 to work on. Give them time to explore the different ways that the problems could be solved and then choose the best way. Once they have done this, ask each group to present their dilemma and their solutions to the group. Ask the group to vote on which one they would choose and then see if this was the same one as the group chose.

RESOURCES

1. Maths puzzles

2. Social dilemmas

3. Pictures of famous women who have supported or helped others, e.g. Edith Cavell, Marie Curie, Mary Seacole, Mother Teresa, Clara Barton, Elizabeth Garrett Anderson

4. *Have You Filled a Bucket Today?* by Carol McCloud and David Messing

IMPORTANT POINTS

Helping and thinking about others is important to society.

LEARNING LINKS

Teamwork, friendships, self-development, emotional literacy.

REFLECTION

Questions:

Positive comment from child:

Positive comment from adult:

LEARNING DIMENSIONS		SOCIAL & EMOTIONAL SKILLS	
Strategic awareness	🟧	Emotional literacy	
Learning relationships		Neuroscience	
Curiosity		Self-regulation	
Creativity	🟩	Self-development	🟩
Meaning making	🟧		
Changing & learning	🟩		
Resilience			

SOCIAL DILEMMA RECORD SHEET

Social Dilemma

Possible Solutions

Solution Choice and Reason

Bibliography

Ainsworth, M. I. S., & Wittig, B. A. (1969). 'Attachment and the exploratory behaviour of one-year-olds in a strange situation.' In B. M. Foss (ed.), *Determinants of Infant Behaviour* (Vol. 4, pp. 113–136). London: Methuen.

Ainsworth, M. D., Bell, S. M., & Stayton, D. J. (1971). 'Individual differences in strange-situation behaviour of one-year-olds.' In H. R. Schaffer, *The Origins of Human Social Relations*. Oxford: Academic Press.

Ainsworth, M. D. S., Blehar, M. C., Waters, E., & Wall, S. N. (2015). *Patterns of Attachment: A Psychological Study of the Strange Situation*. New York: Psychology Press.

'Being assertive 1', by the Samaritans, www.youtube.com/watch?v=n-IfXVpliUI (accessed 3 April 2019).

Bion, W. R. (1963). *Elements of Psycho-analysis*. London: William Heinemann Medical Books Ltd.

Bowlby, J. (1951). *Maternal Care and Mental Health* (Vol. 2). Geneva: World Health Organization.

'Brain games – eyewitness inaccuracy, source monitoring error, and misinformation effect', www.youtube.com/watch?v=RWO2UQ4MW7U (accessed 3 April 2019).

'Critique and feedback – the story of Austin's butterfly', www.youtube.com/watch?v=hqh1MRWZjms (accessed 3 April 2019).

'Cup stacking – team building exercise', www.youtube.com/watch?v=S-MTuGSTJR8 (accessed 3 April 2019).

De Lestrade, A. and Docampo, V. (2010). *Phileas's Fortune: A Story about Self-expression*. Washington, DC: Magination Press.

'Flexibility and accepting input from others in play', www.youtube.com/watch?v=KW53r14o9UE (accessed 3 April 2019).

'For the Birds' animation, www.youtube.com/watch?v=IK13SWOQWO4 (accessed 3 April 2019).

Frankel, E. (2015). *Nobody!: A Story about Overcoming Bullying in Schools*. Minneapolis, MN: Free Spirit Publishing.

Geddes, H. (1999). 'Attachment and learning: An investigation into links between maternal attachment experience, reported life events, behaviour causing concern at referral and difficulties in learning', PhD thesis, Roehampton Institute at the University of Surrey.

Geddes, H. (2006). *Attachment in the Classroom: A Practical Guide for Schools.* London: Worth Publishing.

'Giving and receiving feedback – course trailer', www.youtube.com/watch?v=Qg7jZVJuDE0 (accessed 3 April 2019).

Gould, S. J. (1992). *Ever Since Darwin: Reflections in Natural History.* London: W. W. Norton & Co.

Greder, A. (2008). *The Island.* Sydney: Allen and Unwin.

Helsley, D. (2011). *The Day No-one Played Together: A Story about Compromise.* Fort Payne, AL: Mirror Publishing.

'How can I be more creative? Exercise cognitive flexibility with a mini creative thinking workshop', www.youtube.com/watch?v=c3vOdKONMsA (accessed 3 April 2019).

'How to read body language', www.youtube.com/watch?v=Nmp_-JByPaY (accessed 3 April 2019).

Klein, M. (1931). 'A contribution to the theory of intellectual inhibition', *The International Journal of Psychoanalysis*, 12, 206–218.

Könnecke, O. (2015). *You Can Do It, Bert!* Wellington, New Zealand: Gecko Press.

Koppens, J. (2019). *A Kiss for Giraffe.* New York: Clavis.

McCain, B. R. (2017). *Nobody Knew What to Do.* Park Ridge, IL: Albert Whitman and Company.

McCloud, C. and Messing, D. (2015). *Have You Filled a Bucket Today?* Brighton, MI: Bucket Fillers.

Mantchev, L. (2016). *Strictly No Elephants.* London: Simon and Schuster/Paula Wiseman Books.

Minuchin, P. P., & Shapiro, E. K. (1983). 'The school as a context for social development.' In Paul H. Mussen (ed.) *Handbook of Child Psychology*, Vol. 4. New York: John Wiley.

Moses, B. (1998). *I Don't Care: Learning about Respect.* London: Wayland Publishers.

'Motivational speech', www.youtube.com/watch?v=DjCLbtUOL3A (accessed 3 April 2019).

Mr Bean, 'Shopping with Bean', www.youtube.com/watch?v=6IIPvYGex2s (accessed 3 April 2019).

Mr Bean, 'Sandwich for lunch', www.youtube.com/watch?v=jtqpuYvOfHY (accessed 3 April 2019).

'Nonverbal communication', www.youtube.com/watch?v=csaYYpXBCZg (accessed 3 April 2019).

Olson, K. (2014). *The Invisible Classroom: Relationships, Neuroscience & Mindfulness in School* (The Norton Series on the Social Neuroscience of Education). London: W. W. Norton & Company.

Otoshi, K. (2014). *Two*. Mill Valley, CA: Ko Kids Books.

Pett, M. and Rubinstein, G. (2012). *The Girl Who Never Made Mistakes*. Naperville, IL: Sourcebooks Kids.

'Puppy walking video', www.youtube.com/watch?v=e651783C6_o (accessed 3 April 2019).

'Quick teaching tip: Feedback', www.youtube.com/watch?v=SYXgMobMU8U (accessed 3 April 2019).

Raschka, C. (2013). *Everyone Can Learn to Ride a Bicycle*. Random House Inc.

'Real stories proving you should never give up', www.youtube.com/watch?v=ILcGPGteSGg (accessed 3 April 2019).

'Resilience in kids', www.youtube.com/watch?v=HYsRGeOtfZc (accessed 3 April 2019).

'Resilient – best motivation video', www.youtube.com/watch?v=PdjHG_bGKhk&pbjreload=10 (accessed 3 April 2019).

Resnick, M. D., Bearman, P. S., Blum, R. W., Bauman, K. E., Harris, K. M., Jones, J., . . . & Ireland, M. (1997). 'Protecting adolescents from harm: Findings from the National Longitudinal Study on Adolescent Health', *Jama*, 278(10), 823–832.

Roberton, F. (2016). *The Tale of Two Beasts*. Hodder Children's Books.

Salzberger-Wittenberg, I., Henry, G. & Osborne, E. (1983). *The Emotional Experience of Learning and Teaching*. London: Routledge & Kegan Paul.

Schore, A. N. (1994). *Affect Regulation and the Origin of the Self*. Hillsdale, NJ and Hove, UK: Lawrence Erlbaum Associates.

'Sesame Street: Grover and Zachary Quinto are flexible', www.youtube.com/watch?v=LTryB5 5xbbY&list=PL2IaUn5FkXCJhWCgMNjfOsQrgneVU41om (accessed 3 April 2019).

Shepherd, J. (2018). *The Unkind Buffalo: Little Stories, Big Lessons*. South Africa: Awareness Publishing.

Siegel, D. J. (2015). *The Developing Mind: How Relationships and the Brain Interact to Shape Who We Are*, Second Edition. New York: Guilford Press.

'Stand in my shoes: Exposing and erasing the empathy deficit', www.kickstarter.com/projects/peacelily/stand-in-my-shoes-exposing-and-erasing-the-empathy (accessed 3 April 2019).

Stott, A. (2018). *Want to Play Trucks*? Somerville, MA: Candlewick Press.

TAIKO Studios (2018). CGI Animated Short Film 'One Small Step' by TAIKO Studios/CGMeetup, www.youtube.com/watch?v=yWd4mzGqQYo (accessed 3 April 2019).

'Test your awareness: Whodunnit?', www.youtube.com/watch?v=ubNF9QNEQLA (accessed 3 April 2019).

'The bystander effect', www.youtube.com/watch?v=Wy6eUTLzcU4 (accessed 3 April 2019).

'The monkey business illusion', www.youtube.com/watch?v=IGQmdoK_ZfY (accessed 3 April 2019).

'The ten most passive aggressive phrases', www.youtube.com/watch?v=1Cr1ztMqdro (accessed 3 April 2019).

'The 35 greatest speeches in history', www.artofmanliness.com/articles/the-35-greatest-speeches-in-history/ (accessed 3 April 2019).

Tomashek, B. and Wade, S. (2016). CGI Animated Short Film HD 'Dust Buddies' by Beth Tomashek & Sam Wade | CGMeetup, www.youtube.com/watch?v=mZ6eeAjgSZI&index=1&list=PLMizheSITLyBew_HdvvzzPFS3X7PBQRbL (accessed 3 April 2019).

'Treasure' by Chelsea Bartlett, www.youtube.com/watch?v=PjgxCZnzGLQ (accessed 3 April 2019).

Waber, B. (2002). *Courage*. Boston: Houghton Mifflin.

Walton, K. J. (2016). *A Muddle of Mistakes*. K. J. Walton.

Watt, M. (2008). *Scaredy Squirrel Makes a Friend*. Toronto: Kids Can Press.

Weber, J. (2016). *Farmer Herman and the Flooding Barn*. Savage, MN: Broadstreet Publishing.

Williams, G. (1997). *Internal Landscapes and Foreign Bodies: Eating Disorders and Other Pathologies*. London: Karnac Books.

Wimmer, S. (2012). *The Word Collector*. Madrid: Cuento De Luz.

Wormell, C. (2008). *The Saddest King*. London: Red Fox Picture Books.